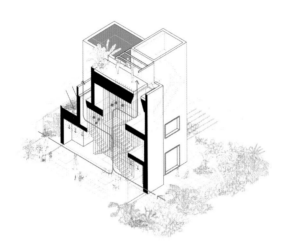

Editorial project:
2021 © **booq** publishing, S.L.
c/ Domènech, 7-9, 2º 1ª
08012 Barcelona, Spain
T: +34 93 268 80 88
www.booqpublishing.com

ISBN 978-84-9936-689-0 [EN]
ISBN 978-84-9936-687-6 [DE]

monsa
publications

2021 © Instituto Monsa de ediciones, S.L.
c/ Gravina, 43
08930 Sant Adrià de Besós,
Barcelona, Spain
T: +34 93 381 00 93
www.monsa.com
monsa@monsa.com

ISBN 978-8417557-40-9

Editorial coordinator:
Claudia Martínez Alonso

Art director:
Mireia Casanovas Soley

Editor:
Daniela Santos Quartino

Layout:
Cristina Simó Perales

Translation:
© **booq** publishing, S.L.

Printing in Spain

Minimalism is the counterpoint to visual, sound and conceptual noise. Its basic principles go back to Chinese Taoism and the Zen philosophy of the 5th century, and its influence on architecture began in the 1920s with the Bauhaus and De Stijl. But the fact is that often it re-emerges with new force as a vital response to the essential.

In times of over stimulation, over information and consumerism, minimalism is a way to calm. Not only as an aesthetic trend, but also as a lifestyle that invites to detachment, to organize, to focus on what is important, and to reduce the unnecessary as much as possible.

In the same way, minimalist constructions induce to leave out the noise of the cities and create a space of meditation, serenity and calm. Thus, the aesthetic trend becomes less dogmatic and embraces new forms inspired by nature and the environment.

Today's minimalist architecture is dominated by harmony, balance, craftsmanship, attention to detail, integration into the landscape and a focus on sustainability.

The decoration focuses on light, monochromatic ranges of earth and raw tones, touch, surfaces and natural materials. It is a cosy and sentimental minimalism in contrast to the purer and more rational 80s and 90s.

The New Minimalist Style echoes these new forms with projects all over the world, which appeal to warmth and calm. The following pages present the latest work of a selection of architects and interior designers who reflect their roots and influences in their work: city flats that express beauty without ostentation; desert residences open to nature; white volumes that cut into the Mediterranean landscape; the Nordic serenity of wood panelling; the raw, textured materials of wabi sabi style. There is also room for the brutalist imprint of exposed concrete that blurs the boundary between indoors and outdoors; midcentury houses converted into sanctuaries of peace; and, in the strict sense, a minimalism of compositional cleanliness through highly defined volumes and refined surfaces.

All these projects share a minimalist DNA, and acquire timelessness. Sites that will always respond to the recurring need for a return to substance.

Der Minimalismus ist der Kontrapunkt zum visuellen, akustischen und konzeptionellen Lärm. Seine Grundprinzipien gehen auf den chinesischen Taoismus und die Zen-Philosophie aus dem 5. Jahrhundert zurück, und sein Einfluss auf die Architektur begann in den 1920er Jahren mit dem Bauhaus und De Stijl. Aber Tatsache ist, dass sie immer wieder mit neuer Kraft als vitale Antwort auf das Wesentliche auftaucht.

In Zeiten der Reizüberflutung, der Informationsflut und des Konsumdenkens ist Minimalismus ein Weg zur Ruhe. Nicht nur als ästhetischer Trend, sondern auch als Lebensstil, der dazu einlädt, Abstand zu nehmen, Ordnung zu schaffen, sich auf das Wesentliche zu konzentrieren und das Unnötige so weit wie möglich zu reduzieren.

Auf die gleiche Weise verleiten minimalistische Bauten dazu, den Lärm der Städte auszublenden und einen Raum der Meditation, Gelassenheit und Ruhe zu schaffen. Die ästhetische Tendenz wird also weniger dogmatisch und umfasst neue Formen, die von der Natur und der Umwelt inspiriert sind.

Die minimalistische Architektur von heute ist geprägt von Harmonie, Ausgewogenheit, Handwerkskunst, Liebe zum Detail, Integration in die Landschaft und Nachhaltigkeit.

Die Dekoration konzentriert sich auf helle, monochromatische Erd- und Rohtöne, Berührungen, Oberflächen und natürliche Materialien. Es ist ein gemütlicher und sentimentaler Minimalismus im Gegensatz zu den reineren und rationaleren 80er und 90er Jahren.

Der New Minimalist Style greift diese neuen Varianten mit Projekten in der ganzen Welt auf, die an Wärme und Ruhe appellieren. Auf den folgenden Seiten werden die neuesten Arbeiten ausgewählter Architekten und Innenarchitekten vorgestellt, die in ihren Werken ihre Wurzeln und Einflüsse widerspiegeln: Stadtwohnungen, die Schönheit ohne Prunk ausdrücken; Wüstenresidenzen, die sich der Natur öffnen; weiße Volumen, die sich in die mediterrane Landschaft einfügen. Die nordische Gelassenheit von Holzvertäfelungen; die rohen, strukturierten Materialien von Wabi Sabi. Es gibt auch Raum für die brutalistische Prägung des Sichtbetons, der die Grenze zwischen Innen und Außen verwischt, für Häuser aus der Mitte des Jahrhunderts, die zu Zufluchtsorten der Ruhe umgewandelt wurden, und für den Stricto-Senso-Minimalismus der kompositorischen Sauberkeit durch genau definierte Volumen und raffinierte Oberflächen.

All diese Projekte haben eine minimalistische DNA und sind zeitlos. Websites, die immer wieder auf das Bedürfnis nach einer Rückkehr zum Wesentlichen reagieren.

Le minimalisme est le contrepoint du bruit visuel, sonore et conceptuel. Ses principes de base remontent au taoïsme chinois et à la philosophie zen du Ve siècle, et son influence sur l'architecture a commencé dans les années 1920 avec le Bauhaus et De Stijl. Mais le fait est qu'elle réapparaît souvent avec une force nouvelle comme une réponse vitale à l'essentiel.

En ces temps de surstimulation, de surinformation et de consumérisme, le minimalisme est un moyen de se calmer. Non seulement comme une tendance esthétique, mais aussi comme un style de vie qui invite au détachement, à l'organisation, à la concentration sur ce qui est important et à la réduction du superflu autant que possible.

De la même manière, les constructions minimalistes incitent à laisser de côté le bruit des villes et à créer un espace de méditation, de sérénité et de calme. Ainsi, la tendance esthétique devient moins dogmatique et embrasse de nouvelles formes inspirées par la nature et l'environnement.

L'architecture minimaliste d'aujourd'hui est dominée par l'harmonie, l'équilibre, l'artisanat, le souci du détail, l'intégration dans le paysage et l'accent mis sur la durabilité.

La décoration se concentre sur des gammes légères et monochromes de tons terreux et bruts, le toucher, les surfaces et les matériaux naturels. C'est un minimalisme douillet et sentimental qui contraste avec les années 80 et 90, plus pures et plus rationnelles.

Le Nouveau Style Minimaliste fait écho à ces nouvelles formes avec des projets dans le monde entier, qui font appel à la chaleur et au calme. Les pages suivantes présentent les dernières réalisations d'une sélection d'architectes et de décorateurs d'intérieur qui reflètent leurs racines et leurs influences dans leur travail : des appartements en ville qui expriment la beauté sans ostentation ; des résidences dans le désert ouvertes sur la nature ; des volumes blancs qui se découpent sur le paysage méditerranéen ; la sérénité nordique des boiseries ; les matériaux bruts et texturés du style wabi sabi. Il y a aussi de la place pour l'empreinte brutaliste du béton apparent qui brouille la frontière entre l'intérieur et l'extérieur ; les maisons du milieu du siècle converties en sanctuaires de paix ; et, au sens strict, un minimalisme de la propreté compositionnelle à travers des volumes très définis et des surfaces raffinées.

Tous ces projets partagent un ADN minimaliste, et acquièrent une intemporalité. Des sites qui répondront toujours au besoin récurrent d'un retour à la substance.

El minimalismo es el contrapunto al ruido visual, sonoro, conceptual. Sus principios básicos se remontan al taoísmo chino y la filosofía zen del siglo V, y su influencia en la arquitectura empezó en los años 20 con la Bauhaus y De Stijl. Pero cada cierto período de tiempo vuelve a irrumpir con nuevas fuerzas como una respuesta vital hacia lo esencial.

En momentos de sobreestimulación, exceso de información y consumismo, el minimalismo es una vía para la calma. No solo como corriente estética, sino además como un estilo de vida que invita al desapego, el orden, a centrarse en lo importante, y a reducir al máximo lo innecesario.

De la misma manera, las construcciones minimalistas inducen a dejar fuera el ruido de las ciudades y crear un espacio de meditación, serenidad y calma. Así, la tendencia estética se vuelve menos dogmática y abraza nuevas formas inspiradas por la naturaleza y el entorno.

En la arquitectura minimalista actual predomina la armonía, el equilibrio, la artesanía, el cuidado de los detalles, la integración en el paisaje y un interés especial por la sostenibilidad.

La decoración se centra en la luz, las gamas monocromáticas de tonos tierras y crudos, el tacto, las superficies y los materiales naturales. Es un minimalismo acogedor y de sentimientos a diferencia de los años 80 y 90, más puro y racional.

The New Minimalist Style se hace eco de estas nuevas variantes con proyectos en todo el mundo, que apelan a la calidez y la calma. En las siguientes páginas, se presentan los últimos trabajos de una selección de arquitectos e interioristas que plasman en su obra sus raíces e influencias: apartamentos en la ciudad que expresan lo bello sin ostentación; residencias en el desierto abiertas a la naturaleza; volúmenes blancos que se recortan en el paisaje mediterráneo. La serenidad nórdica de los revestimientos de madera; los materiales *raw* y texturizados del *wabi sabi*. También tiene cabida la impronta brutalista del hormigón visto que borra la frontera entre interior y exterior; el *mid-century* en casas convertidas en santuarios de sosiego; y el minimalismo *stricto senso* de limpieza compositiva través de volúmenes muy definidos y superficies depuradas.

Todos estos proyectos comparten un ADN minimalista, y adquieren la atemporalidad. Sitios que siempre responderán a la necesidad recurrente de un retorno hacia lo sustancial.

Adrian Chan Design & Research Office (ADRO) is an interior design studio that incorporates aesthetic refinement and optimisation of use into its designs. He has completed commercial and residential projects in the United States and Hong Kong, conditioned by a humanistic, wellness-oriented approach and a local and international contextual narrative. Its design philosophy is the fusion of form and function, drawing references from fields as diverse as fine art, business, neuro-aesthetics and pop culture. Chan founded ADRO in New York in 2018. Prior to founding his studio, he held positions at international architecture firms, designing five-star hotels and resorts, luxury housing, offices and university buildings. He holds a master's degree in interior design from Pratt Institute, a GD from Chelsea College of Art and a bachelor's degree from the University of Pennsylvania.

Adrian Chan Design & Research Office (ADRO) ist ein Innenarchitekturbüro, das in seinen Entwürfen ästhetische Raffinesse und Nutzungsoptimierung vereint. Er hat in den Vereinigten Staaten und in Hongkong kommerzielle und Wohnprojekte realisiert, die von einem humanistischen, wellnessorientierten Ansatz und einem lokalen und internationalen Kontext geprägt sind. Seine Designphilosophie ist die Verschmelzung von Form und Funktion, wobei er Referenzen aus so unterschiedlichen Bereichen wie der bildenden Kunst, der Wirtschaft, der Neuroästhetik und der Popkultur zieht. Chan gründete ADRO im Jahr 2018 in New York. Bevor er sein Studio gründete, war er in internationalen Architekturbüros tätig und entwarf Fünf-Sterne-Hotels und -Resorts, Luxuswohnungen, Büros und Universitätsgebäude. Er hat einen Master-Abschluss in Innenarchitektur vom Pratt Institute, ein GD vom Chelsea College of Art und einen Bachelor-Abschluss von der University of Pennsylvania.

Adrian Chan Design & Research Office (ADRO) est un studio de design d'intérieur qui intègre dans ses créations le raffinement esthétique et l'optimisation de l'utilisation. Il a réalisé des projets commerciaux et résidentiels aux États-Unis et à Hong Kong, conditionnés par une approche humaniste, axée sur le bien-être, et un récit contextuel local et international. Sa philosophie de conception est la fusion de la forme et de la fonction, puisant ses références dans des domaines aussi divers que les beaux-arts, les affaires, la neuro-esthétique et la culture pop. Chan a fondé ADRO à New York en 2018. Avant de fonder son studio, il a occupé des postes dans des cabinets d'architecture internationaux, concevant des hôtels et des complexes hôteliers cinq étoiles, des logements de luxe, des bureaux et des bâtiments universitaires. Il est titulaire d'un master en design d'intérieur du Pratt Institute, d'un GD du Chelsea College of Art et d'une licence de l'université de Pennsylvanie.

Adrian Chan Design & Research Office (ADRO) es un estudio de interiorismo que incorpora a sus diseños el refinamiento estético y la optimización del uso. Ha completado proyectos comerciales y residenciales en los Estados Unidos y en Hong Kong, condicionados por una mirada humanista, de bienestar y una narrativa contextual local e internacional. Su filosofía de diseño es la fusión de la forma y la función, y toma referencias de campos tan diversos como las bellas artes, los negocios, la neuro estética y la cultura pop. Chan creó ADRO en Nueva York en el 2018. Antes de fundar su estudio, ocupó puestos en firmas internacionales de arquitectura, en el diseño de hoteles y resorts de cinco estrellas, viviendas de lujo, oficinas y edificios universitarios. Cuenta con un máster en diseño de interiores por el Pratt Institute, un GD del Chelsea College of Art y una licenciatura por la Universidad de Pensilvania.

ADRIAN CHAN DESIGN & RESEARCH OFFICE (ADRO)

ADRIAN CHAN

NEW YORK, UNITED STATES
HONG KONG
WWW.ADROFFICE.COM

LONGITUDINAL STUDIO TOKYO

TOKYO, JAPAN

Photos © Adrian Chan

This one-bedroom, longitudinal-shaped studio is a typical first-floor bachelor flat. The owner purchased this 44 m² flat because of its potential for vacation rental, as it is located in the heart of the vibrant Ginza District.

The flat is conceived as a sequence of linear and interconnected spaces, which arouse different sensations. From the "expectation" of the entrance, it moves to "awakening" in the kitchen and dining room, and culminates in "comfort" in the bedroom and living room. Visually, the adjoining rooms are framed with an Escherian wall, which generates views from both sides. The wall itself is a homage to Neo Art Deco.

In keeping with the mandates of minimalism, special attention has been paid to optimising storage for an uncluttered and functional space. The east-facing panel is an expanding cupboard that houses the necessities of daily life: food, cleaning products and equipment, entertainment, clothing and furniture (including a folding dining table). The kitchen, meanwhile, conceals all but the basics, such as the hob and sink.

Dieses längliche Studio mit einem Schlafzimmer ist eine typische Junggesellenbude im ersten Stock. Der Eigentümer erwarb diese 44 Quadratmeter große Wohnung wegen ihres Potenzials zur Ferienvermietung, da sie sich im Herzen des pulsierenden Ginza-Viertels befindet.

Die Wohnung ist als eine Abfolge von linearen und miteinander verbundenen Räumen konzipiert, die unterschiedliche Empfindungen hervorrufen. Von der „Erwartung" im Eingangsbereich geht es zum „Erwachen" in der Küche und im Esszimmer und gipfelt im „Komfort" im Schlafzimmer und im Wohnzimmer. Optisch werden die angrenzenden Räume von einer Escherschen Wand eingerahmt, die Ausblicke von beiden Seiten ermöglicht. Die Wand selbst ist eine Hommage an das Neo Art Deco.

Im Sinne des Minimalismus wurde besonderes Augenmerk auf die Optimierung des Stauraums gelegt, um einen aufgeräumten und funktionalen Raum zu schaffen. Das nach Osten ausgerichtete Paneel ist ein sich ausdehnender Schrank, in dem die Dinge des täglichen Lebens untergebracht sind: Lebensmittel, Reinigungsmittel und -geräte, Unterhaltung, Kleidung und Möbel (darunter ein klappbarer Esstisch). In der Küche hingegen ist nur das Nötigste vorhanden, wie Kochfeld und Spüle.

Ce studio d'une chambre à coucher de forme longitudinale est une garçonnière typique du premier étage. Le propriétaire a acheté cet appartement de 44 m² en raison de son potentiel de location de vacances, car il est situé au cœur du quartier animé de Ginza.

L'appartement est conçu comme une séquence d'espaces linéaires et interconnectés, qui suscitent différentes sensations. De l'« attente » de l'entrée, on passe à l'« éveil » dans la cuisine et la salle à manger, pour aboutir au « confort » dans la chambre et le salon. Visuellement, les pièces contiguës sont encadrées par un mur escherien, qui génère des vues des deux côtés. Le mur lui-même est un hommage au néo-art déco.

Conformément aux exigences du minimalisme, une attention particulière a été accordée à l'optimisation du rangement pour un espace épuré et fonctionnel. Le panneau orienté vers l'est est un placard extensible qui abrite les nécessités de la vie quotidienne : nourriture, produits et équipements de nettoyage, divertissement, vêtements et meubles (y compris une table à manger pliante). La cuisine, quant à elle, dissimule tout sauf l'essentiel, comme la plaque de cuisson et l'évier.

Este estudio de una sola habitación y forma longitudinal es el típico primer piso que se compra un soltero. El propietario adquirió este apartamento de 44 m², por su potencial para el alquiler vacacional, ya que se encuentra en el corazón del vibrante Distrito de Ginza.

La vivienda está pensada como una secuencia de espacios lineales e interconectados, que despiertan sensaciones diferentes. De la «expectativa» de la entrada, se pasa al «despertar» en la cocina y el comedor, y se culmina con el «confort» en el dormitorio y el salón. Visualmente, los ambientes adjuntos están enmarcados con un muro Escheriano, que genera vistas desde ambos lados. La pared como tal, es un homenaje al Neo Art Decó.

Siendo fiel a los mandatos del minimalismo, se ha puesto especial atención en optimizar el almacenamiento para obtener un espacio despejado y funcional. El panel que da hacia el Este es un armario que se expande y alberga lo necesario para la vida diaria: alimentos, productos y equipos de limpieza, entretenimiento, ropa y muebles (incluida una mesa de comedor abatible). La cocina por su parte, oculta todo excepto lo básico, como los fogones y el fregadero.

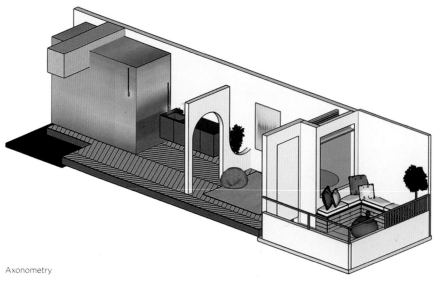

Axonometry

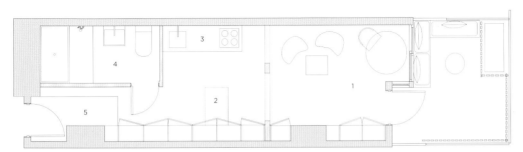

Floor plan

1. Living room / bedroom
2. Dining
3. Kitchen unit
4. Bathroom
5. Genkan

OFFICE OF BLOCKS

HONG KONG

Photos © Kevin Mak

The client for this project is an HR and financial advisory firm that needed an office that was attractive, versatile, and focused on the very specific needs of its staff. The office was to accommodate team meetings —from 4 to 18 people— and training activities. But the space had some drawbacks, the ceilings were low and the size was limited (41 m^2).

The solution is a minimalist structure of elongated strips that draw attention to the horizontal, with the cabinets made up of floating functional blocks installed on a peripheral wall. Each block serves an essential purpose, "'stationery and printing" or "food and drink", and is celebrated as an aesthetic curiosity. The remaining areas allow for flexible uses and maximise spatial efficiency.

To enhance the sense of openness requested by the client, the aesthetic incorporates warm, textured and light finishes, with a rich use of light oak, copper and *calacatta* marble.

Der Kunde für dieses Projekt ist ein Personal und Finanzberatungsunternehmen, das ein attraktives, vielseitiges Büro benötigte, das auf die ganz speziellen Bedürfnisse seiner Mitarbeiter ausgerichtet ist. Das Büro sollte für Teamsitzungen - von 4 bis 18 Personen - und Schulungsmaßnahmen genutzt werden. Aber der Raum hatte einige Nachteile. Die Decken waren niedrig und die Größe war begrenzt (41 Quadratmeter).

Die Lösung ist eine minimalistische Struktur aus länglichen Streifen, die die Aufmerksamkeit auf die Horizontale lenken. Die Schränke bestehen aus schwebenden Funktionsblöcken, die an einer Außenwand installiert sind. Jeder Block dient einem wesentlichen Zweck, sei es „Schreibwaren und Druck" oder „Essen und Trinken", und wird als ästhetische Kuriosität gefeiert. Die verbleibenden Flächen ermöglichen flexible Nutzungen und maximieren die räumliche Effizienz.

Um das vom Kunden gewünschte Gefühl der Offenheit zu verstärken, wurde die Ästhetik durch warme, strukturierte und helle Oberflächen mit reichlich hellem Eichenholz, Kupfer und Calacatta-Marmor ergänzt.

Le client de ce projet est une société de conseil en ressources humaines et en finances qui avait besoin d'un bureau attrayant, polyvalent et axé sur les besoins très spécifiques de son personnel. Le bureau devait accueillir des réunions d'équipe - de 4 à 18 personnes - et des activités de formation. Mais l'espace présentait quelques inconvénients, les plafonds étaient bas et la taille était limitée (41 m^2).

La solution est une structure minimaliste de bandes allongées qui attirent l'attention sur l'horizontale, les armoires étant constituées de blocs fonctionnels flottants installés sur un mur périphérique. Chaque bloc sert un objectif essentiel, « papeterie et impression » ou « nourriture et boisson », et est célébré comme une curiosité esthétique. Les zones restantes permettent des utilisations flexibles et maximisent l'efficacité spatiale.

Pour renforcer le sentiment d'ouverture demandé par le client, l'esthétique incorpore des finitions chaudes, texturées et légères, avec une utilisation riche de chêne clair, de cuivre et de marbre calacatta.

El cliente de este proyecto es una firma de Recursos Humanos y consultoría financiera que necesitaba una oficina atractiva, versátil, y centrada en una necesidades muy específicas de su personal. El despacho debía permitir alojar encuentros del equipo de trabajo, de 4 a 18 personas, y actividades de formación. Pero el espacio presentaba algunos inconvenientes. Los techos eran bajos y el tamaño limitado (41 m^2).

La solución que se planteó es una estructura minimalista de bandas alargadas que dirigen la atención hacia lo horizontal. Los armarios están conformados por bloques funcionales flotantes instalados en una pared periférica. Cada bloque cumple un propósito esencial, ya sea «papelería e impresión» o «comida y bebida», y se celebra como una curiosidad estética. Las áreas restantes permiten usos flexibles y maximizan la eficiencia espacial.

Para potenciar la sensación de apertura solicitada por el cliente, la estética incorpora acabados cálidos, texturizados y ligeros, con abundante uso de roble claro, cobre y mármol *calacatta*.

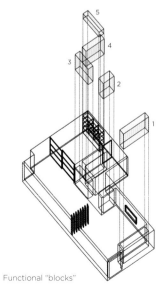

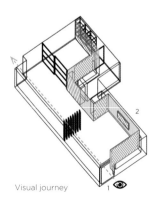

Functional "blocks"

1. General filing
2. Coffee bar / pantry
3. Stationary & printing booth
4. It & office equipment
5. Corporate documents

Visual journey

1. Sight-line to outdoors
2. Gallery wall of blocks

From a shared interest in exploring design from a wide range of scales, programs and disciplines, partners Joshua Aidlin and David Darling started Aidlin Darling Design around a woodworking shop in 1997. The award-winning studio acts as a creative hub for a network of collaborators, including artists, builders, craftspeople, engineers and chefs, with a firm belief that design can enlighten the human spirit by engaging all the senses.

Since its origination, Aidlin Darling Design has collected more than 200 regional, national and international awards, including the inaugural AIA/COTE Top Ten Plus Green Project Award, two international Civic Trust Awards, seven national AIA Awards and two James Beard Awards. In 2013, the firm received the Smithsonian's Cooper-Hewitt Museum's National Design Award for all of its work.

Die Partner Joshua Aidlin und David Darling gründeten Aidlin Darling Design 1997 in einer Holzwerkstatt aus dem gemeinsamen Interesse heraus, Design in verschiedenen Maßstäben, Programmen und Disziplinen zu erforschen. Das preisgekrönte Studio fungiert als kreativer Knotenpunkt für ein Netzwerk von Mitarbeitern, darunter Künstler, Bauunternehmer, Handwerker, Ingenieure und Köche, in der festen Überzeugung, dass Design den menschlichen Geist erleuchten kann, indem es alle Sinne anspricht.

Seit seiner Gründung hat Aidlin Darling Design mehr als 200 regionale, nationale und internationale Auszeichnungen erhalten, darunter den ersten AIA/COTE Top Ten Plus Green Project Award, zwei internationale Civic Trust Awards, sieben nationale AIA Awards und zwei James Beard Awards. Im Jahr 2013 erhielt das Unternehmen den National Design Award des Smithsonian Cooper-Hewitt Museum für alle seine Arbeiten.

Partant d'un intérêt commun pour l'exploration du design à partir d'un large éventail d'échelles, de programmes et de disciplines, les partenaires Joshua Aidlin et David Darling ont créé Aidlin Darling Design autour d'un atelier de menuiserie en 1997. Le studio primé fait office de centre de création pour un réseau de collaborateurs, dont des artistes, des constructeurs, des artisans, des ingénieurs et des chefs, avec la ferme conviction que le design peut éclairer l'esprit humain en faisant appel à tous les sens.

Depuis sa création, Aidlin Darling Design a récolté plus de 200 prix régionaux, nationaux et internationaux, dont le premier prix AIA/COTE Top Ten Plus Green Project, deux prix internationaux Civic Trust, sept prix nationaux AIA et deux prix James Beard. En 2013, le cabinet a reçu le National Design Award du Smithsonian's Cooper-Hewitt Museum pour l'ensemble de son travail.

A partir de un interés compartido por explorar el diseño desde una amplia gama de escalas, programas y disciplinas, los socios Joshua Aidlin y David Darling iniciaron Aidlin Darling Design en torno a un taller de carpintería en 1997. El galardonado estudio actúa como un centro creativo para una red de colaboradores, incluyendo artistas, constructores, artesanos, ingenieros y chefs, con la firme convicción de que el diseño puede iluminar el espíritu humano al involucrar todos los sentidos.

Desde su creación, Aidlin Darling Design ha recogido más de 200 premios regionales, nacionales e internacionales, entre ellos el primer premio AIA/COTE Top Ten Plus Green Project, dos premios internacionales Civic Trust, siete premios nacionales AIA y dos premios James Beard. En 2013, la firma recibió el Premio Nacional de Diseño del Museo Cooper-Hewitt del Smithsonian por toda su obra.

AIDLIN DARLING DESIGN

DAVID DARLING, JOSHUA AIDLIN

CALIFORNIA, UNITED STATES
WWW.AIDLINDARLINGDESIGN.COM

HIGH DESERT RETREAT

CALIFORNIA, UNITED STATES

Photos © Adam Rouse, Joe Fletcher

Situated on a desert plateau on the outskirts of Palm Desert, this single-family residence is perched on a constellation of rocks, overlooking the Coachella Valley and San Jacinto Mountain Range.
The house functions as a minimalist framing device for the occupants to observe the dynamic surrounding terrain, which is the true protagonist. The crisp geometric structure intentionally contrasts with the organic forms of the desert, and is set low to the ground to minimise its presence.
The house has a floating roof plane with an opening that frames the sky and lets the sun into the pool area. A rectilinear set of seven wooden volumes contains the house's programme and slides into the landscape. Two parallel concrete walls frame not only the entrance and dining room, but also the breathtaking views.
The materials of the house were chosen to contrast with the neutral palette of the desert landscape. The blackened timber cladding is of treated pine. The spacious, uncluttered interiors are a collage of concrete, wood, stone and steel surfaces.

Gelegen auf einem wüstenplateau am rande von Palm Desert, thront dieses Einfamilienhaus auf einer Felsenkonstellation mit Blick auf das Coachella Valley und San Jacinto Mountain Range.
Das Haus dient den Bewohnern als minimalistischer Rahmen für die Beobachtung des dynamischen Geländes, das der eigentliche Protagonist ist. Die klare, geometrische Struktur steht in bewusstem Kontrast zu den organischen Formen der Wüste und ist niedrig angesetzt, um ihre Präsenz zu minimieren.
Das Haus hat eine schwebende Dachebene mit einer Öffnung, die den Himmel einrahmt und die Sonne in den Poolbereich lässt. Ein geradliniger Satz von sieben Holzbändern enthält das Programm des Hauses und gleitet in die Landschaft. Zwei parallele Betonwände rahmen nicht nur den Eingang und das Esszimmer ein, sondern auch die atemberaubende Aussicht.
Die Materialien des Hauses wurden so gewählt, dass sie mit der neutralen Farbpalette der Wüstenlandschaft kontrastieren. Die geschwärzte Holzverkleidung ist aus behandelter Kiefer. Die geräumigen, aufgeräumten Innenräume sind eine Collage aus Beton, Holz, Stein und Stahl.

Situé sur un plateau désertique à la périphérie de Palm Desert, cette résidence unifamiliale est perchée sur une constellation de rochers, surplombant la vallée de Coachella et San Jacinto Mountain Range.
La maison fonctionne comme un dispositif de cadrage minimaliste permettant aux occupants d'observer le terrain dynamique environnant, qui est le véritable protagoniste. La structure géométrique nette contraste intentionnellement avec les formes organiques du désert, et est placée bas sur le sol pour minimiser sa présence.
La maison a un toit flottant avec une ouverture qui encadre le ciel et laisse le soleil pénétrer dans la zone de la piscine. Un ensemble rectiligne de sept volumes en bois contient le programme de la maison et se glisse dans le paysage. Deux murs parallèles en béton encadrent non seulement l'entrée et la salle à manger, mais aussi les vues imprenables.
Les matériaux de la maison ont été choisis pour contraster avec la palette neutre du paysage désertique. Le bardage en bois noirci est en pin traité. Les intérieurs spacieux et épurés sont un collage de surfaces en béton, bois, pierre et acier.

Situada en una meseta en el desierto a las afueras de Palm Desert, esta residencia unifamiliar está anclada sobre una constelación de rocas, con vistas al valle de Coachella y San Jacinto Mountain Range.
La casa funciona como un dispositivo de encuadre minimalista para que los ocupantes observen el dinámico terreno circundante, que es el verdadero protagonista. La estructura de geometría nítida, contrasta intencionadamente con las formas orgánicas del desierto, y está situada a ras del suelo para minimizar su presencia.
La casa tiene un plano de cubierta flotante con una abertura que enmarca el cielo y deja pasar el sol en la zona de la piscina. Un conjunto rectilíneo de siete volúmenes de madera contiene el programa de la casa y se desliza hacia el paisaje. Dos muros de hormigón paralelos no sólo enmarcan la entrada y el comedor, sino también, las impresionantes vistas.
Los materiales de la vivienda se eligieron para contrastar con la paleta neutra del paisaje desértico. El revestimiento de madera ennegrecida es de pino tratado. Los interiores, amplios y despejados, son un *collage* de superficies en cemento, madera, piedra y acero.

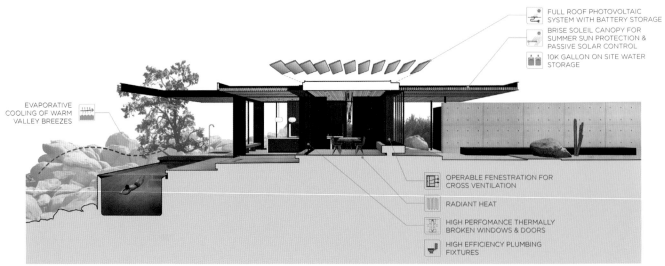

FULL ROOF PHOTOVOLTAIC
SYSTEM WITH BATTERY STORAGE

BRISE SOLEIL CANOPY FOR
SUMMER SUN PROTECTION &
PASSIVE SOLAR CONTROL

10K GALLON ON SITE WATER
STORAGE

EVAPORATIVE
COOLING OF WARM
VALLEY BREEZES

OPERABLE FENESTRATION FOR
CROSS VENTILATION

RADIANT HEAT

HIGH PERFOMANCE THERMALLY
BROKEN WINDOWS & DOORS

HIGH EFFICIENCY PLUMBING
FIXTURES

Sectional sustainability diagram

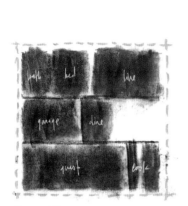

Charcoal Diagram

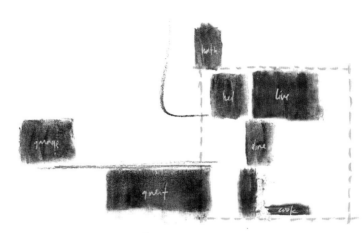

Atelierco is an architectural firm based in Tokyo, established in 2015 by Taishin Shiozaki and Saeco Kobayashi which main focus is the implementation of creative projects, from objects to urban planning proposals.

Recent awards include the Japan Wood Design Award 2020 for its Gohira House and the SD Review 2018 for Pit-House in Kikuna.

Founding partner Taishin Shiozaki completed his studies at the Tokyo Institute of Technology, where he is currently an associate professor, and at Delft University of Technology in the Netherlands. Partner Saeco Kobayashi is a graduate of Tokyo University of Science and a visiting professor at the Nippon Institute of Technology.

Atelierco ist ein Architekturbüro mit Sitz in Tokio, das 2015 von Taishin Shiozaki und Saeco Kobayashi gegründet wurde. Der Schwerpunkt des Unternehmens liegt auf der Umsetzung kreativer Projekte, von Objekten bis hin zu städtebau- lichen Entwürfen.

Zu den jüngsten Auszeichnungen gehören der Japan Wood Design Award 2020 für das Gohira House und der SD Re- view 2018 für Pit House en Kikuna.

Der Gründungspartner Taishin Shiozaki schloss sein Studium am Tokyo Institute of Technology - wo er derzeit außeror- dentlicher Professor ist - und an der Delft University of Technology in den Niederlanden ab. Partner Saeco Kobayashi ist Absolvent der Tokyo University of Science und Gastprofessor an der Nippon Institute of Technology.

Atelierco est un cabinet d'architecture basé à Tokyo, créé en 2015 par Taishin Shiozaki et Saeco Kobayashi dont l'objectif principal est la mise en œuvre de projets créatifs, des objets aux propositions d'urbanisme.

Parmi les récompenses récentes, citons le Japan Wood Design Award 2020 pour sa Gohira House et la SD Review 2018 pour le Pit House in Kikuna.

L'associé fondateur Taishin Shiozaki a terminé ses études à l'Institut de technologie de Tokyo, où il est actuellement professeur associé, et à l'Université de technologie de Delft aux Pays-Bas. L'associé Saeco Kobayashi est diplômé de l'Université des sciences de Tokyo et professeur invité à le Nippon Institute of Technology.

Atelierco es un estudio de arquitectura con sede en Tokio, creado en el año 2015 por Taishin Shiozaki y Saeco Kobayashi. El principal interés de esta firma es la implementación de proyectos creativos, desde objetos hasta propuestas de pla- nificación urbana.

Entre las distinciones que ha obtenido recientemente se cuenta el Japan Wood Design Award 2020, por su proyecto Gohira House, y el SD Review 2018 por Pit House en Kikuna.

El socio fundador Taishin Shiozaki completó sus estudios en el Instituto de Tecnología de Tokio —donde actualmente es profesor adjunto— y en la Universidad de Tecnología de Delft, en los Países Bajos. Por su parte, la socia Saeco Kobayashi, egresada de la Universidad de Ciencia de Tokio, es profesora en el Nippon Institute of Technology.

ATELIERCO

TAISHIN SHIOZAKI, SAECO KOBAYASHI

TOKYO, JAPAN
WWW.ATORIECO.INFO

BRASS HOUSE

TOKYO, JAPAN

Photos © Jumpei Suzuki

The house is built in a densely populated residential neighbourhood in Somei Komagome, an area known as the birthplace of the Somei-Yoshino cherry tree. The owner wanted a house with open spaces but enough privacy. Combining such contradictory directions was a great challenge for the architects because the property was flanked by buildings on both sides. Fortunately, however, there were open spaces to the front and rear. The silhouette of the house is based on two roofs: one in the centre of the façade and one in the centre of the building. With symmetry in mind, the south elevation is designed in the form of a gable-roofed house. There, an imaginary cross-section divides the façade into two halves. One side is completely open, revealing the interior of the building, while the other conceals it. It was not possible to juxtapose the areas with different uses under the two roofs. But the two spaces complement each other. The large window on the façade lets in the light that floods the open-plan interiors. The smooth surfaces in cement and wood, in neutral and white tones, provide the sensation of the openness desired by the owners.

Das Haus steht in einem dicht besiedelten Wohnviertel in Somei Komagome, einer Gegend, die als Geburtsort des Somei-Yoshino-Kirschbaums bekannt ist. Der Eigentümer wünschte sich ein Haus mit offenen Räumen, aber ausreichend Privatsphäre. Die Kombination dieser widersprüchlichen Richtungen war eine große Herausforderung für die Architekten, da das Grundstück auf beiden Seiten von Gebäuden flankiert wurde. Zum Glück gab es aber vorne und hinten freie Flächen. Die Silhouette des Hauses basiert auf zwei Dächern: einem in der Mitte der Fassade und einem in der Mitte des Gebäudes. Mit Blick auf die Symmetrie ist die Südfassade in Form eines Giebeldachs gestaltet. Dort teilt ein imaginärer Querschnitt die Fassade in zwei Hälften. Eine Seite ist völlig offen und gibt den Blick auf das Innere des Gebäudes frei, während die andere Seite es verdeckt. Es war nicht möglich, die Bereiche mit unterschiedlicher Nutzung unter den beiden Dächern nebeneinander zu stellen. Aber die beiden Räume ergänzen sich gegenseitig. Das große Fenster an der Fassade lässt das Licht in die offen gestalteten Innenräume strömen. Die glatten Oberflächen aus Zement und Holz in neutralen und weißen Farbtönen vermitteln das von den Eigentümern gewünschte Gefühl der Offenheit.

La maison est construite dans un quartier résidentiel densément peuplé de Somei Komagome, une zone connue comme le lieu de naissance du cerisier Somei-Yoshino. Le propriétaire souhaitait une maison avec des espaces ouverts mais suffisamment d'intimité. Combiner des orientations aussi contradictoires a été un grand défi pour les architectes, car la propriété était flanquée de bâtiments des deux côtés. Heureusement, il y avait des espaces ouverts à l'avant et à l'arrière. La silhouette de la maison repose sur deux toits : un au centre de la façade et un au centre du bâtiment. Dans un souci de symétrie, l'élévation sud est conçue sous la forme d'une maison à toit à pignon. Là, une coupe transversale imaginaire divise la façade en deux moitiés. Un côté est complètement ouvert, révélant l'intérieur du bâtiment, tandis que l'autre le dissimule. Il n'était pas possible de juxtaposer les zones à usage différent sous les deux toits. Mais les deux espaces se complètent. La grande fenêtre de la façade laisse entrer la lumière qui inonde les espaces intérieurs ouverts. Les surfaces lisses en ciment et en bois, dans des tons neutres et blancs, donnent la sensation d'ouverture souhaitée par les propriétaires.

La casa está construida en un barrio residencial muy densamente poblado en Somei Komagome, una zona que se conoce como la cuna del cerezo Somei-Yoshino. El propietario anhelaba una vivienda con espacios abiertos, pero suficiente privacidad. Combinar direcciones tan contradictorias supuso un gran reto para los arquitectos porque la propiedad estaba flanqueada por edificios a ambos lados. Aunque afortunadamente contaba con espacios abiertos por delante y detrás. La silueta de la vivienda se basa en dos tejados: uno en el centro de la fachada y otro en el centro del edificio. Teniendo en cuenta la simetría, el alzado sur está diseñado en forma de casa con tejado a dos aguas. Allí, un corte transversal imaginario divide la fachada en dos mitades. Uno de los flancos está completamente abierto y muestra el interior de la construcción, mientras que el otro lo oculta. No fue posible yuxtaponer las áreas con diferentes usos bajo los dos tejados. Pero ambos espacios se complementan. El gran ventanal de la fachada deja pasar la luz que inunda los ambientes interiores diáfanos. Las superficies lisas en cemento y madera, en tonos neutros y blancos, terminan de aportar esa sensación de apertura tan deseada por los propietarios.

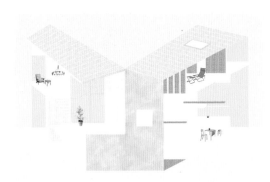

Section image

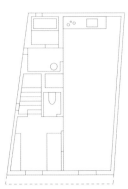

First floor plan

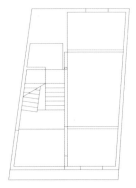

Second floor plan

Third floor plan

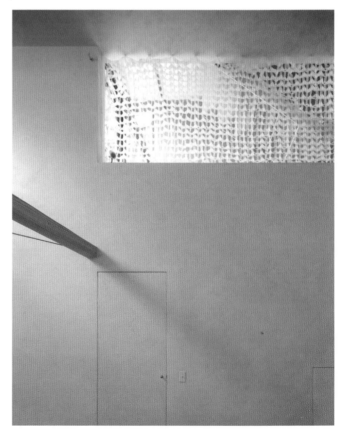

HOUSE IN KAMI-IKEBUKURO

TOKYO, JAPAN

Photos © Jumpei Suzuki, Chika Kato, Atelierco

This house in a high-density residential area is built for three families, each living on one level. Although the inhabitants of the house are related, they wanted to live independently. On the whole, the different levels are separate, but they all breathe the same atmosphere.

The house has a cubic shape of 10 x 10 x 10 m. The outer concrete wall has a gate silhouette on each side of the façade, and is planned as a structural wall. The floor, covered with concrete slabs, rests on a grid beam struc- ture free of columns.

The floating floor screed is coupled to the geometrically shaped objects in the perimeter area. Many of the vis- ually connected vertical spaces feature superimposed figures. Each floor is basically one space with a main concrete structure under the grid beams.

The interior walls and furniture are made of wood and remain separate from the concrete walls. Both physical and visual geometries are superimposed in the perimeter area with the intention of opening up to the sur- rounding urban space.

Dieses Haus in einem Wohngebiet mit hoher Bevölkerungsdichte wurde für drei Familien gebaut, die jeweils auf einer Ebene leben. Obwohl die Bewohner des Hauses miteinander verwandt sind, wollten sie unabhängig voneinander leben. Im Großen und Ganzen sind die verschiedenen Ebenen unabhängig, aber sie atmen alle die gleiche Atmosphäre.

Das Haus hat eine kubische Form von zehn Metern mal zehn Metern mal zehn Metern. Die äußere Betonwand hat auf jeder Seite der Fassade eine Türsilhouette und ist als Strukturwand geplant. Der mit Betonplatten be- deckte Boden ruht auf einer Gitterträgerkonstruktion. Es gibt also keine Spalten.

Der schwimmende Estrich ist im Randbereich mit der geometrisch geformten Wand verbunden. So sind viele der visuell verbundenen vertikalen Räume mit übereinanderliegenden Figuren versehen. Jedes Stockwerk ist im Grunde ein einziger Raum mit einer Hauptbetonstruktur unter den Gitterträgern.

Die Innenwände und Möbel sind aus Holz und bleiben von den Betonwänden getrennt. Sowohl physische als auch visuelle Geometrien überlagern sich im Randbereich mit der Absicht, sich zum umgebenden Stadtraum zu öffnen.

Cette maison située dans un quartier résidentiel à forte densité est construite pour trois familles, chacune vi- vant sur un niveau. Bien que les habitants de la maison soient apparentés, ils souhaitaient vivre de manière in- dépendante. Dans l'ensemble, les différents niveaux sont séparés, mais ils respirent tous la même atmosphère.

La maison a une forme cubique de 10 x 10 x 10 m. Le mur extérieur en béton a une silhouette de grand porte de chaque côté de la façade, et est prévu comme un mur structurel. Le plancher, recouvert de dalles de béton, repose sur une structure de poutres en treillis dépourvue de colonnes.

La chape flottante du plancher est couplée au mur de forme géométrique dans la zone périphérique. De nombreux espaces verticaux reliés visuellement présentent des figures superposées. Chaque étage est essen- tiellement un espace avec une structure principale en béton sous les poutres de la grille.

Les murs intérieurs et le mobilier sont en bois et restent séparés des murs en béton. Des géométries physiques et visuelles sont superposées dans la zone périphérique dans le but de s'ouvrir à l'espace urbain environnant

Esta casa en una zona residencial de alta densidad está construida para tres familias, cada una de las cuales vive en un nivel. Pese a que los habitantes de la casa están vinculados por parentesco, querían vivir de forma autónoma. En conjunto, los diferentes niveles son independientes, pero todos respiran una misma atmósfera.

La vivienda tiene una forma cúbica de 10 x 10 x 10 m. La pared exterior de cemento cuenta con una silueta de portal en cada lado de la fachada, y se ha planificado como un muro estructural. El suelo, revestido con losas de cemento, descansa sobre una estructura de vigas de cuadrícula. Por tanto, no hay columnas.

El pavimento flotante del suelo se acopla a la pared con formas geométricas en la zona perimetral. Así, muchos de los espacios verticales visualmente conectados presentan figuras superpuestas. Cada planta es básicamente un espacio con una estructura principal de cemento bajo las vigas de rejilla.

Las paredes interiores y el mobiliario son de madera y permanecen separados de los muros de cemento. Tan- to las geometrías físicas como las visuales se superponen en la zona perimetral con la intención de apertura hacia el espacio urbano circundante.

Exterior slab

Second floor

Third floor

First floor plan

Second floor plan

Third floor plan

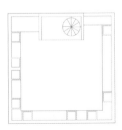

Roof top plan

BETA.Ø is a firm based in Madrid, which develops its professional activity in the areas of architecture, urban planning, landscape architecture and design. Founded by Borja Peña in 2000, it grew in 2015 with the incorporation of partners Ernesto Sierra and Xabier Ortega. Since its creation, the firm has won a long list of awards and distinctions.

Their maxim is knowing how to understand the place, the integration between function and form, understanding the industrial processes of materials as part of the design, sustainability and respect for the environment. The work of these architects is defined by a constant search for sustainable and avant-garde construction materials, techniques and technologies.

BETA.Ø ist ein Büro mit Sitz in Madrid, das seine berufliche Tätigkeit in den Bereichen Architektur, Stadtplanung, Landschaftsarchitektur und Design entfaltet. Das Unternehmen wurde im Jahr 2000 von Borja Peña gegründet und wuchs 2015 durch die Aufnahme der Partner Ernesto Sierra und Xabier Ortega. Seit seiner Gründung hat das Unternehmen eine lange Liste von Preisen und Auszeichnungen erhalten.

Ihre Maxime ist das Verständnis für den Ort, die Integration von Funktion und Form, das Verständnis für die industriellen Prozesse der Materialien als Teil des Designs, die Nachhaltigkeit und der Respekt für die Umwelt. Die Arbeit dieser Architekten ist geprägt von einer ständigen Suche nach nachhaltigen und innovativen Baumaterialien, Techniken und Technologien.

BETA.Ø est un cabinet basé à Madrid, qui développe son activité professionnelle dans les domaines de l'architecture, de l'urbanisme, de l'architecture du paysage et du design. Fondé par Borja Peña en 2000, il s'est développé en 2015 avec l'incorporation des associés Ernesto Sierra et Xabier Ortega. Depuis sa création, le cabinet a remporté une longue liste de prix et de distinctions.

Leur maxime est de savoir comprendre le lieu, l'intégration entre la fonction et la forme, la compréhension des processus industriels des matériaux dans le cadre de la conception, la durabilité et le respect de l'environnement. Le travail de ces architectes se définit par une recherche constante de matériaux, de techniques et de technologies de construction durables et avant-gardistes.

BETA.Ø es una firma con sede en Madrid, que desarrolla su actividad profesional en las áreas de arquitectura, planeamiento urbano, paisajismo y diseño. Fundada por Borja Peña en el año 2000, crece en el año 2015, con la incorporación de los socios Ernesto Sierra y Xabier Ortega. Desde su creación, el despacho cuenta en su haber con una larga lista de premios y distinciones.

Su máxima es saber entender el lugar, la integración entre la función y la forma, comprender los procesos industriales de los materiales como parte del diseño, la sostenibilidad y el respeto al medioambiente. El trabajo de estos arquitectos se define por una búsqueda constante de materiales, técnicas y tecnologías de construcción sostenibles y de vanguardia.

BETA.Ø
ARCHITECTURE OFFICE

BORJA PEÑA, ERNESTO SIERRA, XABIER ORTEGA

MADRID, SPAIN
WWW.BETA-PUNTOCERO.COM

X.Ø HOUSE

MADRID, SPAIN

Photos © Imagen Subliminal, David Zarzoso

This semi-detached house is located in the exclusive area of El Viso, a neighbourhood with villas and gardens in the centre of Madrid. Given its location, one of the objectives was to bring the exterior into the interior of the house. To this end, several terraces were designed to take advantage of the building's staggered layout and large windows.

The design prioritises natural lighting and cross ventilation. The vertical communication of the house is resolved with a light, suspended metal structure that colonises the central space. The industrial-style finishes unify the interior and exterior environments. Continuous cement and compacted chipboard flooring, exposed concrete slabs, steel and glass contrast with the lighting´s warmth, the unvarnished wood of the furniture and the built-in joinery. The space and the careful selection of materials contribute to filtering natural energy, storing and redistributing it to achieve optimum interior thermal comfort. In addition, water was incorporated into the roof and geothermal wells were installed to optimise the energy performance of the new building.

Diese Doppelhaushälfte befindet sich in der exklusiven Gegend von El Viso, einem Viertel mit Villen und Gärten im Zentrum von Madrid. In Anbetracht der Lage des Hauses bestand eines der Ziele darin, den Außenbereich in das Innere des Hauses zu bringen. Zu diesem Zweck wurden mehrere aufeinanderfolgende Terrassen angelegt, um die gestaffelte Anordnung des Gebäudes und die großen Fenster zu nutzen.

Bei der Gestaltung wurde der natürlichen Beleuchtung und der Querlüftung Vorrang eingeräumt. Die vertikale Kommunikation des Hauses wird durch eine leichte, abgehängte Metallstruktur gelöst, die den zentralen Raum besiedelt. Die im industriellen Stil gehaltenen Oberflächen vereinen die Innen- und Außenbereiche. Durchgehende Zement- und Pressspanböden, Sichtbetonplatten, Stahl und Glas kontrastieren mit der Wärme des hellen, unlackierten Holzes der Möbel und der eingebauten Tischlerarbeiten. Der Raum und die sorgfältige Auswahl der Materialien tragen dazu bei, die natürliche Energie zu filtern, zu speichern und umzuverteilen, um einen optimalen thermischen Komfort im Inneren zu erreichen. Um die Energiebilanz des neuen Gebäudes zu optimieren, wurden außerdem Wasser in das Dach integriert und geothermische Brunnen installiert.

Cette maison mitoyenne est située dans la zone exclusive d'El Viso, un quartier de villas et de jardins au centre de Madrid. Compte tenu de son emplacement, l'un des objectifs était de faire entrer l'extérieur à l'intérieur de la maison. À cette fin, plusieurs terrasses ont été conçues pour tirer parti de la disposition en quinconce du bâtiment et de ses grandes fenêtres.

La conception donne la priorité à l'éclairage naturel et à la ventilation croisée. La communication verticale de la maison est résolue par une structure métallique légère et suspendue qui colonise l'espace central. Les finitions de style industriel unifient les environnements intérieur et extérieur. Les sols en ciment continu et en aggloméré compacté, les dalles de béton apparent, l'acier et le verre contrastent avec la chaleur de l'éclairage, le bois non verni des meubles et les menuiseries intégrées. L'espace et le choix judicieux des matériaux contribuent à filtrer l'énergie naturelle, à la stocker et à la redistribuer pour obtenir un confort thermique intérieur optimal. De plus, l'eau a été incorporée dans la toiture et des puits géothermiques ont été installés pour optimiser la performance énergétique du nouveau bâtiment.

Esta vivienda unifamiliar pareada se sitúa en la exclusiva zona de El Viso, un barrio con chalets y jardines en el centro de Madrid. Dada su situación, uno de los objetivos era llevar el exterior al interior de la vivienda. Para ello se proyectaron varias terrazas sucesivas que aprovechan el escalonamiento del edificio y amplios ventanales.

El diseño prioriza la iluminación natural y la ventilación cruzada. La comunicación vertical de la casa se resuelve con una estructura metálica ligera y suspendida que coloniza el espacio central. Los acabados de tipo industrial unifican los ambientes interiores y exteriores. Suelo continuo de tableros de cemento y viruta compactada, losas de hormigón visto, acero y vidrio, contrastan con la calidez de la madera clara y sin barnizar del mobiliario y la carpintería empotrada. El espacio y la cuidada selección de materiales contribuye a filtrar la energía natural, almacenándola y redistribuyéndola para conseguir el óptimo confort térmico interior. Además, para optimizar el rendimiento energético del nuevo edificio, se incorporó agua en la cubierta y se instalaron pozos geotérmicos.

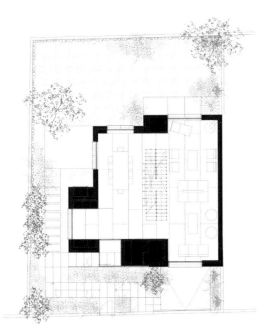

Ground floor plan

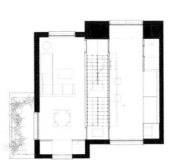

First floor plan

Second floor plan

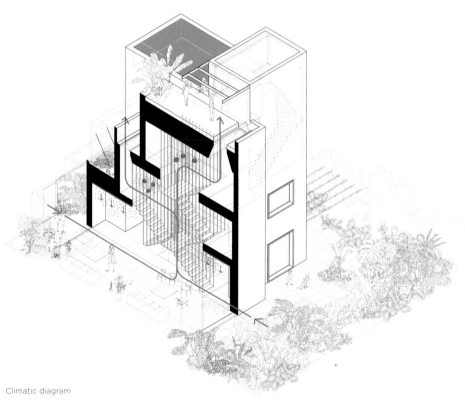

Climatic diagram

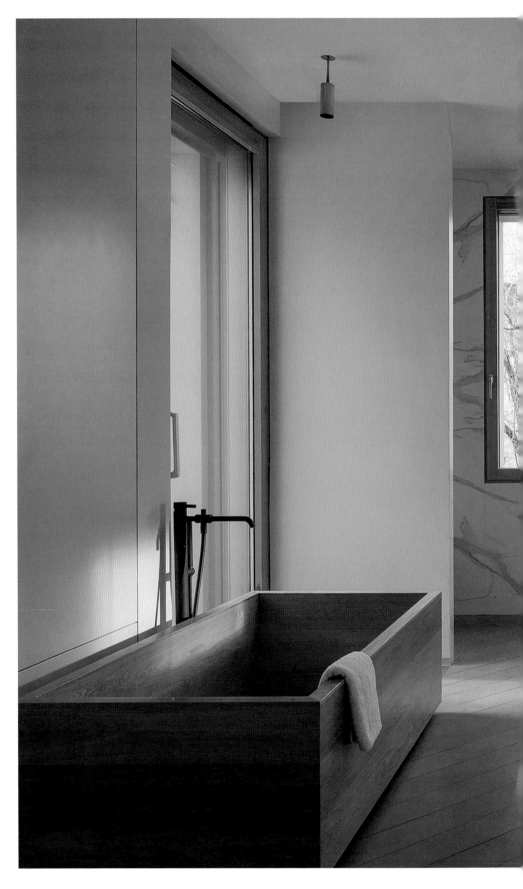

U.Ø HOUSE

MADRID, SPAIN

Photos © David Zarzoso

This house, located on the Paseo de la Castellana in Madrid, is the product of a renovation to extend and optimise the uses of the original space. The interior design project created open and flexible areas. A system of lightweight enclosures made it possible to compartmentalise the rooms of the house without breaking the visual flow or obstructing the entry of natural light. The living room, dining room and kitchen can be separated from the rest of the house to become a meeting or work area. The integration of the rooms is reinforced by the use of large-format materials on the floor, such as long wooden planks or stone pieces in the dining and kitchen areas. The design of the enclosures refers to the forms of traditional Mediterranean architecture. The introduction of a curved decorative motif creates an attractive perspective in the straight-lined environment that dominates the interior of the house. The noble materials of the finishes and furnishings, such as black and grey-green stone and natural oak wood, are combined with the delicate tones of copper and bronze to give the house a sense of calm and character.

Dieses Haus am Paseo de la Castellana in Madrid ist das Ergebnis einer Renovierung, bei der die ursprünglichen Räumlichkeiten erweitert und optimal genutzt wurden. Das Innenarchitekturprojekt schuf offene und flexible Bereiche. Ein System von leichten Schränken ermöglichte es, die Räume des Hauses zu unterteilen, ohne den visuellen Fluss zu unterbrechen oder den Einfall von natürlichem Licht zu behindern. Das Wohnzimmer, das Esszimmer und die Küche können vom Rest des Hauses abgetrennt werden, um als Besprechungs- oder Arbeitsbereich zu dienen. Die Integration der Räume wird durch die Verwendung von großformatigen Materialien auf dem Boden, wie z.B. langen Holzdielen oder Steinstücken im Esszimmer und Küchenbereich, verstärkt. Die Gestaltung der Gehege nimmt Bezug auf die Formen der traditionellen mediterranen Architektur. Die Einführung eines geschwungenen dekorativen Motivs schafft eine attraktive Perspektive in der geradlinigen Umgebung, die das Innere des Hauses dominiert. Die edlen Materialien der Oberflächen und der Einrichtung, wie schwarzer und graugrüner Stein und natürliches Eichenholz, werden mit den zarten Tönen von Kupfer und Bronze kombiniert, um dem Haus ein Gefühl von Ruhe und Charakter zu verleihen.

Cette maison, située sur le Paseo de la Castellana à Madrid, est le produit d'une rénovation visant à étendre et optimiser les utilisations de l'espace d'origine. Le projet d'aménagement intérieur a permis de créer des zones ouvertes et flexibles. Un système de fermetures légères a permis de compartimenter les pièces de la maison sans rompre le flux visuel ni obstruer l'entrée de la lumière naturelle. Le salon, la salle à manger et la cuisine peuvent être séparés du reste de la maison pour devenir un espace de réunion ou de travail. L'intégration des pièces est renforcée par l'utilisation de matériaux de grand format au sol, tels que de longues planches de bois ou des morceaux de pierre dans la salle à manger et la cuisine. Le design des clôtures fait référence aux formes de l'architecture méditerranéenne traditionnelle. L'introduction d'un motif décoratif incurvé crée une perspective attrayante dans l'environnement rectiligne qui domine l'intérieur de la maison. Les matériaux nobles des finitions et de l'ameublement, tels que la pierre noire et gris-vert et le bois de chêne naturel, sont associés aux tons délicats du cuivre et du bronze pour donner à la maison un sentiment de calme et de caractère.

Esta vivienda ubicada en el Paseo de la Castellana de Madrid, es producto de una reforma para ampliar y optimizar los usos del espacio original. El proyecto de diseño interior creó zonas abiertas y flexibles. Un sistema de cerramientos ligeros, permitió compartimentar los ambientes de la casa sin romper la fluidez visual, ni obstaculizar la entrada luz natural. La sala de estar, el comedor y la cocina se pueden independizar del resto de la vivienda para convertirse en área de reunión o de trabajo. La integración de los ambientes se refuerza con el uso de materiales de gran formato en el suelo, como largos tablones de madera o piezas de piedra en la zona del comedor y la cocina. El diseño de los cerramientos remite a las formas de la arquitectura tradicional mediterránea. La introducción de un motivo decorativo curvo genera una perspectiva atractiva en el entorno de líneas rectas que predominan en el interior de la casa. Los materiales nobles de los acabados y el mobiliario, como la piedra negra y gris verdoso, y la madera de roble natural, se combinan con los tonos delicados del cobre y el bronce y consiguen imprimir calma y carácter a la casa.

Brigita Bula Architects practices considerate and long-lasting architecture for green and future-minded people and organisations. The studio emphasizes ecological and sustainable design and construction practices. Site specific, minimalist aesthetics with refined details, industrial finishes and bold geometry define the architect's work. "We put nature in the center and consider human as a part of it. We look to mould our work to the environment and tradition, and not to mould surrounding nature and site specifics to our needs and instant whims," says the firm's founder. Before opening her architecture studio in 2013, Brigita Bula worked at Arhis design studio in Latvia. On different projects and competitions she has collaborated with different architectural studios in Scotland, the Netherlands and Portugal. The award-winning studio received its most recent distinction in 2019 with the National Architecture Award in Latvia for its Salt house project in Pavilosta. As a national entrant, the project was nominated for the 2020 Mies van der Rohe Award.

Brigita Bula Architects entwirft rücksichtsvolle und dauerhafte architektur für umweltbewusste und zukunftsorientierte menschen und organisationen. Das studio legt den schwerpunkt auf ökologische und nachhaltige design und baupraktiken. Ortsspezifische, minimalistische ästhetik mit raffinierten details, industriellen oberflächen und kühner geometrie bestimmen die arbeit der architekten. „Wir stellen die natur in den mittelpunkt und betrachten den menschen als einen teil von ihr. Wir versuchen, unsere arbeit an die umwelt und die tradition anzupassen und nicht die umgebende natur und die besonderheiten des ortes nach unseren bedürfnissen und momentanen launen zu formen", sagt die gründerin des büros. Bevor sie 2013 ihr architekturbüro eröffnete, arbeitete Brigita Bula im designbüro Arhis in Latvia. Bei verschiedenen Projekten und Wettbewerben hat sie mit verschiedenen Architekturbüros in Schottland, den Niederlanden und Portugal zusammengearbeitet. Die jüngste auszeichnung erhielt das preisgekrönte studio 2019 mit dem Nationalen Architekturpreis in Lettland für sein hausprojekt salt in Pavilosta. Als nationaler teilnehmer wurde das projekt für den Mies van der Rohe Award 2020 nominiert.

Brigita Bula Architects pratique une architecture réfléchie et durable pour des personnes et des organisations soucieuses de l'environnement et de l'avenir. Le studio met l'accent sur les pratiques de conception et de construction écologiques et durables. Le travail de l'architecte se caractérise par une esthétique minimaliste, adaptée au site, avec des détails raffinés, des finitions industrielles et une géométrie audacieuse. « Nous plaçons la nature au centre et considérons que l'homme en fait partie. Nous cherchons à mouler notre travail à l'environnement et à la tradition, et non à mouler la nature environnante et les spécificités du site à nos besoins et à nos caprices instantanés », déclare la fondatrice du cabinet. Avant d'ouvrir son studio d'architecture en 2013, Brigita Bula a travaillé au studio de design Arhis à Latvia. Sur différents projets et concours, elle a collaboré avec différents studios d'architecture en Écosse, aux Pays-Bas et au Portugal. Le studio primé a reçu sa dernière distinction en 2019 avec le prix national d'architecture en Lettonie pour son projet de maison Salt à Pavilosta. En tant que participant national, le projet a été nommé pour le prix Mies van der Rohe 2020.

Brigita Bula Architects hace hincapié en las prácticas de diseño y construcción ecológicas y sostenibles. La estética minimalista y específica del lugar, con detalles refinados, acabados industriales y una geometría audaz, definen el trabajo de la arquitecta. «Ponemos la naturaleza en el centro y consideramos al ser humano como parte de ella. Buscamos amoldar nuestro trabajo al entorno y a la tradición, y no moldear la naturaleza circundante y las particularidades del lugar a nuestras necesidades y caprichos instantáneos», dice la fundadora del estudio. Antes de abrir su firma en 2013, Brigita Bula trabajó en el estudio de diseño Arhis de Latvia. También colaboró en proyectos y firmas de arquitectura de Escocia, Holanda y Portugal. En 2019 el estudio recibió el Premio Nacional de Arquitectura de Letonia por su proyecto de la Salt House en Pavilosta. Como participante nacional, el proyecto fue nominado para el Premio Mies van der Rohe 2020.

BRIGITA BULA ARHITEKTI

BRIGITA BULA

RIGA, LATVIA
WWW.BULA.LV

SALT HOUSE

PĀVILOSTA, LATVIA

Photos © Reinis Hofmanis, Valters Videnieks (aerophoto), Sintija Gadiga (garden photos)

The one-storey 240 m² house is set in a seaside meadow on the edge of town's historical center. It's a simple elongated volume that draws a seawave-like line in the surrounding undulating landscape, leaving as small an imprint in the existing biotope as possible. The lively flowerbed in the front of the house is made by selecting local plants, herbs and flowers from the surounding meadows. The cross-section was inspired by traditional fishermen's houses. Interior opens to the house's full height and width, open and closed spaces overlap, providing a semi-transparent space of both openness and intimacy. The house reminds of a sand dune that catches all the salt carried by the sea breeze. This idea is reflected in the natural material of the facade, similar in its structure and colour to the coarse salt. Pāvilosta has a temperate climate and strong wind, so the building is constructed with thick lime-plastered blocks, with no additional insulation necessary. Surfaces are left without any decorative finishing to expose the essence and natural beauty of the construction materials and technologies. The building will retain its elegance and beauty as it ages —cracks or leaks of rust will fit its image, because this is simply the natural order of things.

Das einstöckige, 240 m² große haus befindet sich auf einer wiese am meer am rande des historischen zentrums der stadt. Es ist ein einfaches, langgestrecktes volumen, das sich wie eine meereswelle in die umgebende hügelige landschaft einfügt und so wenig wie möglich in das bestehende biotop eingreift. Für das lebendige blumenbeet vor dem haus wurden lokale pflanzen, kräuter und blumen von den umliegenden wiesen ausgewählt. Der innenraum öffnet sich über die gesamte höhe und breite des hauses, offene und geschlossene räume überschneiden sich, so dass ein halbtransparenter raum entsteht, der sowohl offenheit als auch intimität ausstrahlt. Das haus erinnert an eine sanddüne, die alles salz auffängt, das die meeresbrise mit sich bringt. Diese idee spiegelt sich in dem natürlichen material der fassade wider, das in seiner struktur und farbe dem groben salz ähnelt. Da in Pāvilosta ein gemäßigtes klima herrscht und der wind stark weht, wurde das gebäude aus dicken, mit kalk verputzten blöcken errichtet, so dass keine zusätzliche isolierung erforderlich ist. Die oberflächen werden ohne jegliche dekorative veredelung belassen, um das wesen und die natürliche schönheit der baumaterialien und -technologien hervorzuheben. Das gebäude wird im laufe der zeit seine eleganz und schönheit bewahren - risse oder undichter rost werden zu seinem image passen, denn das ist einfach die natürliche ordnung der dinge.

La maison d'un étage de 240 m² est située dans une prairie de bord de mer, en bordure du centre historique de la ville. C'est un volume simple et allongé qui dessine une ligne semblable à une vague de mer dans le paysage vallonné environnant, laissant une empreinte aussi faible que possible dans le biotope existant. Le parterre vivant à l'avant de la maison a été réalisé en sélectionnant des plantes, des herbes et des fleurs locales dans les prairies environnantes. L'intérieur s'ouvre sur toute la hauteur et la largeur de la maison, les espaces ouverts et fermés se chevauchent, offrant un espace semi-transparent à la fois ouvert et intime. La maison rappelle une dune de sable qui capte tout le sel transporté par la brise marine. Cette idée se reflète dans le matériau naturel de la façade, similaire dans sa structure et sa couleur au gros sel. Pāvilosta ayant un climat tempéré et un vent fort, le bâtiment est construit avec des blocs épais enduits à la chaux, sans qu'aucune isolation supplémentaire ne soit nécessaire. Les surfaces sont laissées sans finition décorative afin d'exposer l'essence et la beauté naturelle des matériaux et des technologies de construction. Le bâtiment conservera son élégance et sa beauté en vieillissant - les fissures ou les fuites de rouille seront à son image, car c'est tout simplement l'ordre naturel des choses.

La casa, de una sola planta y 240 m², está situada junto al mar, dentro de los límites del centro histórico de la ciudad. Se trata de un sencillo volumen alargado que dibuja una línea similar a la de las olas del mar en el ondulado paisaje circundante. El animado parterre de la parte delantera de la casa se ha realizado seleccionando plantas, hierbas y flores locales. El interior se abre a toda la altura y anchura de la casa, los espacios abiertos y cerrados se superponen, proporcionando un espacio semitransparente de apertura e intimidad a la vez. La casa recuerda a una duna de arena que atrapa toda la sal que lleva la brisa del mar. Esta idea se refleja en el material natural de la fachada, similar en su estructura y color a la sal gruesa. Pāvilosta tiene un clima templado y fuertes vientos, por lo que el edificio está construido con gruesos bloques enlucidos de cal, sin necesidad de aislamiento adicional. Las superficies se deja sin ningún acabado decorativo para exponer la esencia y la belleza natural de los materiales y las tecnologías de construcción.

Location plan

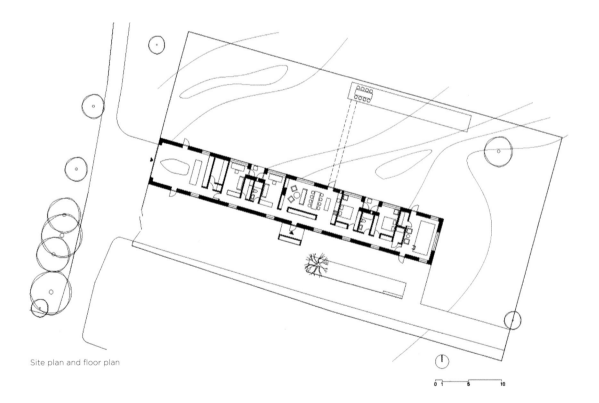

Site plan and floor plan

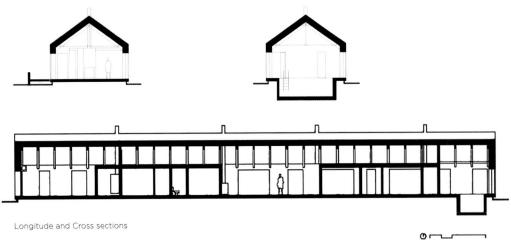

Longitude and Cross sections

Brosh Architects specialises in residential design, reusing existing spaces and maximising their potential. The firm, founded by Lior Brosh, has extensive experience working with period buildings and believes that it is possible to conserve and integrate them into modern living while respecting heritage.

A graduate of Robert Gordon University in Aberdeen, Scotland in 2004, Brosh moved to London after graduation and worked as a project architect at several award-winning firms before setting up his own practice in 2012.

"I didn't discover architecture at a very young age, it was more like architecture that found me. I remember a walk along the banks of the Thames in the 1990s after the renovation of the OXO Tower and its surroundings. That was the moment when I understood the effect of good architecture and design, and its direct and positive impact on our lives," says the architect.

Brosh Architects hat sich auf die Gestaltung von Wohngebäuden, die Wiederverwendung vorhandener Räume und die Maximierung ihres Potenzials spezialisiert. Das von Lior Brosh gegründete Unternehmen verfügt über umfangreiche Erfahrungen im Umgang mit historischen Gebäuden und ist davon überzeugt, dass es möglich ist, diese zu erhalten und in das moderne Leben zu integrieren, ohne das Erbe zu vernachlässigen.

Brosh schloss 2004 sein Studium an der Robert Gordon University in Aberdeen, Schottland, ab. Nach seinem Abschluss zog er nach London und arbeitete als Projektarchitekt in mehreren preisgekrönten Büros, bevor er 2012 sein eigenes Büro gründete. „Ich habe die Architektur nicht in einem sehr jungen Alter entdeckt, sondern sie hat mich eher gefunden. Ich erinnere mich an einen Spaziergang am Themseufer in den 1990er Jahren nach der Renovierung des OXO-Turms und seiner Umgebung. Das war der Moment, in dem ich die Wirkung von guter Architektur und Design und ihren direkten und positiven Einfluss auf unser Leben verstanden habe", sagt der Architekt.

Brosh Architects est spécialisé dans la conception résidentielle, la réutilisation des espaces existants et l'optimisation de leur potentiel. L'entreprise, fondée par Lior Brosh, a une grande expérience des bâtiments d'époque et pense qu'il est possible de les conserver et de les intégrer dans la vie moderne tout en respectant le patrimoine.

Diplômé de l'université Robert Gordon d'Aberdeen, en Écosse, en 2004, Brosh s'est installé à Londres après son diplôme et a travaillé comme architecte de projet dans plusieurs cabinets primés avant de créer son propre cabinet en 2012.

« Je n'ai pas découvert l'architecture très jeune, c'est plutôt l'architecture qui m'a trouvé. Je me souviens d'une promenade sur les rives de la Tamise dans les années 1990, après la rénovation de la tour OXO et de ses environs. C'est à ce moment-là que j'ai compris l'effet d'une bonne architecture et d'un bon design, et leur impact direct et positif sur nos vies », explique l'architecte.

Brosh Architects está especializado en el diseño residencial, la re utilización de espacios existentes y el máximo aprovechamiento de su potencial. La firma fundada por Lior Brosh, tiene una amplia experiencia trabajando con edificios de época y cree que es posible su conservación e integración en la vida moderna sin dejar de respetar el patrimonio.

Egresado de la Universidad Robert Gordon de Aberdeen (Escocia) en 2004, Brosh se trasladó a Londres tras su graduación y trabajó como arquitecto de proyectos en varias firmas galardonadas antes de crear su propio estudio en 2012.

«No descubrí la arquitectura a una edad muy temprana, fue más bien la arquitectura la que me encontró a mí. Recuerdo un paseo por la orilla del Támesis en los años 90 después de la renovación de la Torre OXO y sus alrededores. Ese fue el momento en el que comprendí el efecto de la buena arquitectura y el diseño, y su impacto directo y positivo en nuestras vidas», señala el arquitecto.

BROSH ARCHITECTS

LIOR BROSH

LONDON, UNITED KINGDOM
WWW.BROSHARCHITECTS.COM

WEST 5 FLAT

LONDON, UNITED KINGDOM

Photos © Ollie Hammick

Clean lines and bright spaces: the client's prerogatives were clear and decisive for the renovation of this property in London's Notting Hill district. The 1930s flat was dark and subdivided into several small rooms. To create more space, some partition walls were removed and full-height doors were installed. One of the walls at the entrance was also replaced with a louvred partition wall that acts as a divider without blocking the light. The atmosphere changed immediately as natural light flooded into the central corridor and hall and was distributed throughout the rooms. To amplify the brightness and generate diaphanous spaces, the entire house was painted in shades of white, highlighting some details of the old construction to maintain its character. The herringbone oak flooring is completely new and was designed in the same size and pattern as the old one. From the application of false ceilings and the installation of indirect lighting systems, the whimsical lines and angles of the structural walls were concealed. In other cases, the numerous corners and gaps in the main walls were used to create shelving and hidden storage areas.

Klare Linien und helle Räume: Die Vorgaben des Bauherrn waren bei der Renovierung dieser Immobilie im Londoner Stadtteil Notting Hill klar und eindeutig. Die Wohnung aus den 1930er Jahren war dunkel und in mehrere kleine Zimmer unterteilt.
Um mehr Platz zu schaffen, wurden einige Trennwände entfernt und raumhohe Türen eingebaut. Eine der Wände im Eingangsbereich wurde ebenfalls durch eine Trennwand mit Lamellen ersetzt, die als Raumteiler fungiert, ohne das Licht zu blockieren. Die Atmosphäre änderte sich sofort, als natürliches Licht in den zentralen Korridor und die Halle flutete und sich in den Räumen verteilte. Um die Helligkeit zu verstärken und durchlässige Räume zu schaffen, wurde das gesamte Haus in Weißtönen gestrichen, wobei einige Details der alten Konstruktion hervorgehoben wurden, um ihren Charakter zu erhalten. Der Fischgrät-Eichenboden ist völlig neu und wurde in der gleichen Größe und mit dem gleichen Muster wie der alte Boden verlegt. Durch das Anbringen von Zwischendecken und die Installation von indirekten Beleuchtungssystemen wurden die skurrilen Linien und Winkel der Strukturwände verdeckt. In anderen Fällen wurden die zahlreichen Ecken und Lücken in den Hauptwänden genutzt, um Regale und versteckte Stauräume zu schaffen.

Lignes épurées et espaces lumineux : les prérogatives du client étaient claires et décisives pour la rénovation de cette propriété située dans le quartier de Notting Hill à Londres. L'appartement des années 1930 était sombre et divisé en plusieurs petites pièces.
Pour créer plus d'espace, certaines cloisons ont été supprimées et des portes pleine hauteur ont été installées. L'un des murs de l'entrée a également été remplacé par une cloison à lamelles qui fait office de séparation sans bloquer la lumière. L'atmosphère a immédiatement changé lorsque la lumière naturelle a envahi le couloir central et le hall et s'est répandue dans toutes les pièces. Pour amplifier la luminosité et générer des espaces diaphanes, l'ensemble de la maison a été peint dans des tons de blanc, mettant en valeur certains détails de l'ancienne construction pour en conserver le caractère. Le parquet en chêne à chevrons est entièrement nouveau et a été conçu dans la même taille et le même motif que l'ancien. L'application de faux plafonds et l'installation de systèmes d'éclairage indirect ont permis de dissimuler les lignes et les angles fantaisistes des murs structurels. Dans d'autres cas, les nombreux coins et interstices des murs principaux ont été utilisés pour créer des étagères et des zones de rangement cachées.

Líneas limpias y espacios luminosos: las prerrogativas del cliente eran claras y determinantes para la renovación de esta propiedad en el barrio londinense de Notting Hill. El piso de los años 1930, era oscuro y estaba subdividido en varias habitaciones pequeñas.
Para ganar amplitud se removieron algunos tabiques, y se instalaron puertas de altura completa. También se reemplazó una de las paredes de la entrada por un tabique de lamas que actúa como divisor sin bloquear el paso de la luz. La atmósfera cambió inmediatamente cuando la luz natural inundó el pasillo central y el hall, distribuyéndose por todas las habitaciones. Para amplificar la claridad y generar espacios diáfanos se pintó toda la vivienda en tonos de blanco destacando algunos detalles de la vieja construcción para mantener su carácter. El suelo de madera de roble con forma de espiga es totalmente nuevo y se diseño del mismo tamaño y patrón que el antiguo. A partir de la aplicación de falsos techos y la instalación de sistemas de luz indirecta se ocultó las líneas y ángulos caprichosos que tenían las paredes estructurales. En otros casos, se aprovechó las numerosas esquinas y huecos que presentaban los muros principales, para crear estanterías y zonas ocultas de almacenaje.

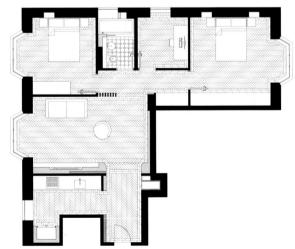

Floor plan (after)

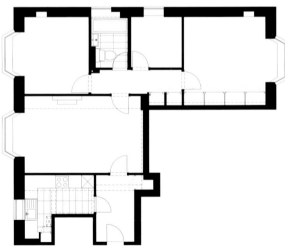

Floor plan (before)

Stephen Bruns founded Bruns Architecture in 2008. Specialising in high quality residential and commercial environments, the firm offers a full range of architectural and design services to manage a project from initial concept and planning through final details, construction administration and furniture design.

The team believes that through careful listening, rigorous study, strong relationships and innovative thinking, the spatial environment can be enhanced by providing thoughtful and enduring architecture.

Bruns Architecture's work explores the power of materiality, texture, detail and light to cultivate meaningful design solutions. Awards include the American Institute of Architects (AIA) of Wisconsin Honor Award and the Association of Licensed Architects (ALA) Design Awards.

Stephen Bruns gründete Bruns Architecture im Jahr 2008. Das Unternehmen hat sich auf hochwertige Wohn- und Geschäftsräume spezialisiert und bietet ein umfassendes Spektrum an Architektur- und Designdienstleistungen an, um ein Projekt vom ersten Konzept und der Planung bis hin zu den endgültigen Details, der Bauverwaltung und dem Möbeldesign zu verwalten.

Das Team ist davon überzeugt, dass durch aufmerksames Zuhören, gründliche Studien, starke Beziehungen und innovatives Denken die räumliche Umgebung durch eine durchdachte und dauerhafte Architektur verbessert werden kann.

Die Arbeit von Bruns Architecture erforscht die Kraft von Materialität, Textur, Details und Licht, um sinnvolle Designlösungen zu entwickeln. Zu den Auszeichnungen gehören der American Institute of Architects (AIA) of Wisconsin Honor Award und die Association of Licensed Architects (ALA) Design Awards.

Stephen Bruns a fondé Bruns Architecture en 2008. Spécialisé dans les environnements résidentiels et commerciaux de haute qualité, le cabinet offre une gamme complète de services d'architecture et de conception pour gérer un projet depuis le concept initial et la planification jusqu'aux détails finaux, l'administration de la construction et la conception du mobilier.

L'équipe est convaincue qu'une écoute attentive, une étude rigoureuse, des relations solides et une pensée innovante permettent d'améliorer l'environnement spatial en proposant une architecture réfléchie et durable.

Le travail de Bruns Architecture explore le pouvoir de la matérialité, de la texture, du détail et de la lumière pour cultiver des solutions de conception significatives. Il a notamment reçu le prix d'honneur de l'American Institute of Architects (AIA) du Wisconsin et les prix de design de l'Association of Licensed Architects (ALA).

Stephen Bruns fundó el estudio Bruns Architecture en 2008. Especializado en entornos residenciales y comerciales de alta calidad, la firma ofrece una gama completa de servicios de arquitectura y diseño para gestionar un proyecto desde el concepto inicial y la planificación hasta los detalles finales, la administración de la construcción y el diseño del mobiliario.

El equipo cree que a través de la escucha atenta, el estudio riguroso, las relaciones sólidas y el pensamiento innovador se puede mejorar el entorno espacial ofreciendo una arquitectura reflexiva y duradera.

El trabajo de Bruns Architecture explora el poder de la materialidad, la textura, el detalle y la luz para cultivar soluciones de diseño significativas. Entre los galardones recibidos se cuenta el Premio de Honor del American Institute of Architects (AIA) de Wisconsin y los Premio de Diseño de la Association of Licensed Architects (ALA).

BRUNS ARCHITECTURE

STEPHEN BRUNS

WISCONSIN, UNITED STATES
WWW.BRUNSARCHITECTURE.COM

WOVEN HOUSE

WISCONSIN, UNITED STATES

Photos © Tricia Shay Photography

Situated on the shores of Lake Winnebago, this home acts as a beacon at the end of a narrow farm road. The design goal was to create a welcoming gathering place for a family of six with a sophisticated sense of style, and to maximise contact with the environment.

The structure is composed of two gabled volumes interlaced by a lower form. In fact, the thickness of the walls was doubled to emphasise the silhouette of the house. The two-storey volume housing the bedrooms is turned towards the lake to amplify the views and harvest additional light.

The palette of finishes plays with contrasts of black and white. The exterior is clad in synthetic slate tiles formulated from recycled tyres. The white stucco chimney punctuates the structure and creates a radiant landmark along the coast.

Inside the house, a restrained palette of materials offers texture and explores variations of neutral tones with accents of black. A rustic cement render covers the walls and ceilings, and reclaimed white oak wood creates a supportive rhythm through the gables.

Am Ufer des Lake Winnebago gelegen, wirkt dieses Haus wie ein Leuchtturm am Ende einer schmalen Farmstraße. Ziel des Entwurfs war es, einen einladenden Treffpunkt für eine sechsköpfige Familie mit einem ausgeprägten Sinn für Stil zu schaffen und den Kontakt zur Umwelt zu maximieren.

Das Gebäude besteht aus zwei giebelständigen Baukörpern, die durch eine niedrigere Form miteinander verbunden sind. Die Dicke der Wände wurde sogar verdoppelt, um die Silhouette des Hauses zu betonen. Das zweigeschossige Volumen, in dem die Schlafzimmer untergebracht sind, ist zum See hin ausgerichtet, um die Aussicht zu verstärken und zusätzliches Licht zu erhalten.

Die Palette der Oberflächen spielt mit Kontrasten von Schwarz und Weiß. Das Äußere ist mit synthetischen Schieferplatten verkleidet, die aus recycelten Reifen hergestellt wurden. Der weiße Stuckschornstein unterstreicht die Struktur und bildet ein strahlendes Wahrzeichen entlang der Küste.

Im Inneren des Hauses bietet eine zurückhaltende Materialpalette Textur und erkundet Variationen von neutralen Tönen mit schwarzen Akzenten. Ein rustikaler Zementputz bedeckt die Wände und Decken, und wiedergewonnenes Weißeichenholz sorgt für einen unterstützenden Rhythmus in den Giebeln.

Située sur les rives du lac Winnebago, cette maison fait office de phare au bout d'une étroite route agricole. L'objectif de la conception était de créer un lieu de rassemblement accueillant pour une famille de six personnes, avec un sens sophistiqué du style, et de maximiser le contact avec l'environnement.

La structure est composée de deux volumes à pignon entrelacés par une forme inférieure. En fait, l'épaisseur des murs a été doublée pour souligner la silhouette de la maison. Le volume de deux étages abritant les chambres est tourné vers le lac pour amplifier les vues et récolter de la lumière supplémentaire.

La palette de finitions joue avec les contrastes de noir et de blanc. L'extérieur est revêtu de tuiles en ardoise synthétique formulées à partir de pneus recyclés. La cheminée en stuc blanc ponctue la structure et crée un point de repère rayonnant le long de la côte.

À l'intérieur de la maison, une palette sobre de matériaux offre de la texture et explore les variations de tons neutres avec des accents de noir. Un enduit de ciment rustique recouvre les murs et les plafonds, et du bois de chêne blanc récupéré crée un rythme de soutien à travers les pignons.

Situada en la orilla del lago Winnebago, esta vivienda actúa como un faro al final de una estrecha carretera agrícola. El objetivo del diseño era crear un lugar de reunión acogedor para una familia de seis personas con un sofisticado sentido del estilo, y maximizar el contacto con el entorno.

La estructura se compone de dos volúmenes a dos aguas entrelazados por una forma más baja. De hecho, se duplicó el grosor de las paredes para enfatizar la silueta de la casa. El volumen de dos plantas que aloja los dormitorios está girado hacia el lago para amplificar las vistas y cosechar luz adicional.

La paleta de acabados juega con contrastes en blanco y negro. El exterior, está revestido con baldosas de pizarra sintética formuladas a partir de neumáticos reciclados. La chimenea de estuco blanco, marca la estructura y crea un punto de referencia radiante a lo largo de la costa.

En el interior de la casa, una restringida paleta de materiales ofrece textura y explora variaciones de tonos neutros con acentos de negro. Un enlucido de cemento rústico cubre las paredes y los techos, y la madera de roble blanco recuperada crea un ritmo de apoyo a través de los hastiales.

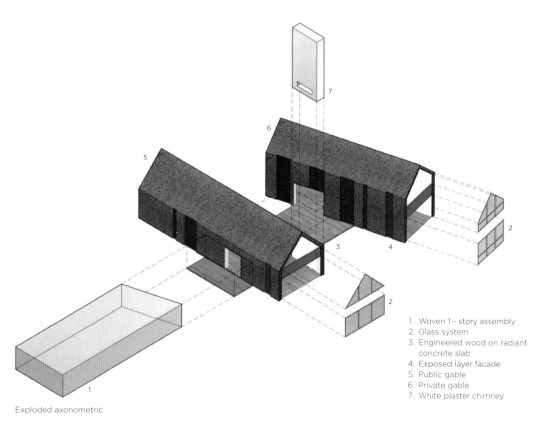

1. Woven 1 - story assembly
2. Glass system
3. Engineered wood on radiant
   concrete slab
4. Exposed layer facade
5. Public gable
6. Private gable
7. White plaster chimney

Exploded axonometric

Chris Briffa completed his architecture degree at the University of Malta in 1999. While attending and organising numerous EASA workshops as a student, he furthered his studies at the Virginia Polytechnic Institute and State University, known as Virginia Tech (USA) and the Politecnico di Milano (Italy). He also collaborated with furniture suppliers and designers in northern Italy before founding his studio in 2004.

His work is synonymous with skilful design that moves away from stylistic mannerisms and is more concerned with proportion, materials and detail. Whether for commercial, residential, public or private purposes, Briffa's vision fuses historic buildings and new spaces. His language is contemporary and multifaceted and integrates passive energy design concerns with simplified elegance.

Chris Briffa schloss 1999 sein Architekturstudium an der Universität von Malta ab. Während er als Student an zahlreichen EASA-Workshops teilnahm und diese organisierte, vertiefte er seine Studien an der Virginia Polytechnic Institute and State University, bekannt als Virginia Tech (USA), und am Politecnico di Milano (Italien). Er arbeitete auch mit Möbellieferanten und Designern in Norditalien zusammen, bevor er 2004 sein Studio gründete.

Sein Werk ist ein Synonym für gekonntes Design, das sich von stilistischen Manierismen entfernt und sich mehr auf Proportionen, Materialien und Details konzentriert. Ob für gewerbliche, private oder öffentliche Zwecke, Briffas Visionen verschmelzen historische Gebäude und neue Räume. Seine Sprache ist zeitgemäß und facettenreich und verbindet die Belange des Passivenergie-Designs mit schlichter Eleganz.

Chris Briffa a obtenu son diplôme d'architecte à l'université de Malte en 1999. Tout en participant et en organisant de nombreux ateliers de l'AESA en tant qu'étudiant, il a poursuivi ses études au Virginia Polytechnic Institute and State University, connu sous le nom de Virginia Tech (États-Unis) et au Politecnico di Milano (Italie). Il a également collaboré avec des fournisseurs de meubles et des designers dans le nord de l'Italie avant de fonder son studio en 2004.

Son travail est synonyme de conception habile qui s'éloigne des maniérismes stylistiques et s'intéresse davantage aux proportions, aux matériaux et aux détails. Que ce soit à des fins commerciales, résidentielles, publiques ou privées, la vision de Briffa fusionne les bâtiments historiques et les nouveaux espaces. Son langage est contemporain et multiforme et intègre les préoccupations de conception de l'énergie passive avec une élégance simplifiée.

Chris Briffa terminó su carrera de arquitectura en la Universidad de Malta en 1999. Mientras asistía y organizaba numerosos talleres de la EASA en su época de estudiante, amplió sus estudios en el Instituto Politécnico y Universidad Estatal de Virginia, conocido como Virginia Tech (Estados Unidos) y el Politécnico de Milán (Italia). También colaboró con proveedores de muebles y diseñadores en el norte de Italia antes de fundar su estudio en 2004.

Su trabajo es sinónimo de un diseño hábil que se aleja de los manierismos estilísticos y se preocupa más por la proporción, los materiales y los detalles. Ya sea para fines comerciales, residenciales, públicos o privados, la visión de Briffa fusiona los edificios históricos y los nuevos espacios. Su lenguaje es contemporáneo y polifacético e integra las preocupaciones de diseño de energía pasiva con una elegancia simplificada.

CHRIS BRIFFA ARCHITECTS

CHRIS BRIFFA

VALETTA, MALTA
WWW.CHRISBRIFFA.COM

CASA BOTTEGA

VALLETTA, MALTA

Photos © Aldo Amoretti

Chris Briffa lived for a time next door to this period house which for years was in an advanced state of dis-repair, before it was offered to him for purchase at a court auction. The attachment and deep experience in working with the limestone, so typical in Malta, are at the heart of this project. The building underwent a multitude of interventions over a period of five years. The lower levels adopted the existing structure with elements such as tiles, openings and textures; and now house the architects' studio. The penthouse however, is a contemporary counterpart, rising above its predecessor and defined by contrasts between soft and hard materials, light and shadow, solids and voids. The extension now houses the architects' family residence. The interior is dominated by open spaces and a neutral cement finish, except in the bedroom where the morning light bounces off an oak floor. The aesthetic success of the extension's façade lies in its undulating surface, cast on a carpet of wooden slats, which gives it an ethereal and light appearance in the sunlight.

Chris Briffa wohnte eine Zeit lang neben diesem historischen Haus. Das Gebäude befand sich in einem fort-geschrittenen Stadium der Verwahrlosung. Doch als der Architekt die Möglichkeit hatte, das Gebäude zu er-steigern, setzte er den Sanierungsprozess in Gang. Die Verbundenheit und die große Erfahrung in der Arbeit mit dem für Malta so typischen Kalkstein sind das Herzstück dieses Projekts. Das Gebäude wurde über einen Zeitraum von fünf Jahren einer Vielzahl von Eingriffen unterzogen. In den unteren Ebenen wurden die vor-handene Struktur und Elemente wie Fliesen, Öffnungen und Texturen übernommen um das Atelier des Archi-tekten unterzubringen. Das Penthouse hingegen ist ein zeitgemäßes Gegenstück, das sich von seinem Vor-gänger abhebt und durch Kontraste zwischen weichen und harten Materialien, Licht und Schatten, Voll- und Hohlräumen bestimmt wird. Der Anbau beherbergt heute das Wohnhaus der Familie. Im inneren dominieren offene räume und eine neutrale zementoberfläche, mit ausnahme des schlafzimmers, in dem das morgenlicht von einem eichenholzboden reflektiert wird. Der ästhetische Erfolg der Fassade des Erweiterungsbaus liegt in ihrer wellenförmigen Oberfläche - gegossen auf einen Teppich aus Holzlatten -, die ihr im Sonnenlicht ein ätherisches und leichtes Aussehen verleiht.

Chris Briffa a vécu un certain temps à côté de cette maison d'époque. Le bâtiment était dans un état de délabre-ment avancé. Mais lorsque l'architecte a eu l'occasion de l'acheter lors d'une vente aux enchères, il a lancé le pro-cessus de réhabilitation. L'attachement et la profonde expérience du travail avec le calcaire, si typique à Malte, sont au cœur de ce projet. Le bâtiment a fait l'objet d'une multitude d'interventions sur une période de cinq ans. Les niveaux inférieurs ont adopté la structure existante et des éléments tels que les tuiles, les ouvertures et les textures pour abriter l'atelier de l'architecte. Le penthouse, quant à lui, est un pendant contemporain, s'éle-vant au-dessus de son prédécesseur et défini par les contrastes entre les matériaux doux et durs, la lumière et l'ombre, les pleins et les vides. L'extension abrite aujourd'hui la résidence familiale. L'intérieur est dominé par des espaces ouverts et une finition neutre en ciment, sauf dans la chambre à coucher où la lumière du matin rebondit sur un plancher en chêne. La réussite esthétique de la façade de l'extension réside dans sa surface ondulée - coulée sur un tapis de lattes de bois - qui lui donne un aspect éthéré et léger à la lumière du soleil.

Chris Briffa vivió durante un tiempo al lado de esta casa de época. El edificio estaba en avanzado estado de abandono. Pero cuando el arquitecto tuvo la oportunidad de comprarlo en una subasta judicial, puso en mar-cha su proceso de rehabilitación. El apego y la profunda experiencia en cómo trabajar con la piedra caliza, tan típica en Malta, son el núcleo de este proyecto. El edificio fue objeto de multitud de intervenciones a lo largo de cinco años. Los niveles inferiores adoptaron la estructura existente, y elementos como azulejos, aberturas y texturas, para albergar el estudio del arquitecto. El ático sin embargo, es una contrapartida contemporánea, que se eleva por encima de su predecesor y se define por los contrastes entre materiales blandos y duros, luz y sombra, sólidos y vacíos. La extensión aloja ahora la residencia familiar. En el interior predominan los ambientes despejados, y un acabado neutro de cemento, excepto en el dormitorio donde la luz de la mañana rebota en el suelo de roble. El éxito estético de la fachada de la ampliación radica en su superficie ondulante —fundida sobre una alfombra de listones de madera— que le da un aspecto etéreo y ligero a la luz del sol.

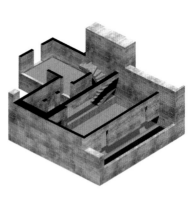
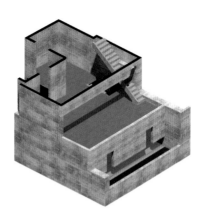
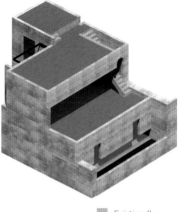

Axonometries

Existing floor
Additional floors
Precast beams

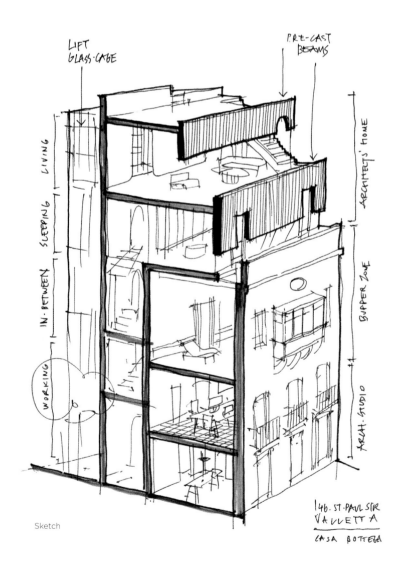

Sketch

100

Penthouse
level one

Penthouse
level two

Penthouse
level three

Roof level

Ground floor plan

First floor plan

Second floor plan

1. Entrance
2. Reception
3. Meeting room
4. Architects' studio
5. Kitchenette
6. Architects' office
7. Bedroom
8. Ensuite
9. Study
10. Kids' bedroom
11. Master bedroom
12. Services area
13. Kitchen
14. Living room
15. Guest WC
16. Roof terrace

Section A-A

Olivier Ottevaere is an architect and teacher whose interest in architecture is based on a hybrid approach between physical experiments and geometric compositions. His projects are based on three lines of interest: the integration of active structural principles, the properties of materials and construction procedures.

He worked in architectural firms in New York, Lisbon and London until co-founding the Double (o) studio in 2012. His research work on prefabrication, "House Me Tender", received the Best Residential Future 2015 award from Architectural Review. He was also a recipient of the Perspective 40 under 40 Asia-Pacific design awards in Architecture. Prior to joining the University of Hong Kong where he is now Associate Professor of Practice, Olivier was a Unit Master at the Architectural Association and has taught design studios at the Royal Academy in Copenhagen as well as at EPFL in Switzerland.

Olivier Ottevaere ist ein Architekt und Lehrer, dessen Interesse an der Architektur auf einem hybriden Ansatz zwischen physikalischen Experimenten und geometrischen Organisationen beruht. Seine Projekte stützen sich auf drei Interessenschwerpunkte: die Integration aktiver Strukturprinzipien, die Eigenschaften der Materialien und die Bauverfahren.

Er arbeitete in Architekturbüros in New York, Lissabon und London, bis er 2012 das Studio Double (o) mitbegründete. Seine Forschungsarbeit zur Vorfertigung, „House me tender", wurde von der Architectural Review mit dem Preis Best Residential Future 2015 ausgezeichnet. Außerdem wurde er mit dem Perspective 40 under 40 Asia-Pacific Design Award in Architektur ausgezeichnet. Bevor er an die Universität von Hongkong kam, wo er jetzt als Associate Professor of Practice tätig ist, war Olivier Unit Master an der Architectural Association und unterrichtete Designstudios an der Royal Academy in Kopenhagen sowie an der EPFL in der Schweiz.

Olivier Ottevaere est un architecte et un enseignant dont l'intérêt pour l'architecture repose sur une approche hybride entre expériences physiques et organisations géométriques. Ses projets s'articulent autour de trois lignes d'intérêt : l'intégration de principes structurels actifs, les propriétés des matériaux et les procédures de construction.

Il a travaillé dans des cabinets d'architectes à New York, Lisbonne et Londres jusqu'à la cofondation du studio Double (o) en 2012. Son travail de recherche sur la préfabrication, « House me tender », a reçu le prix du meilleur avenir résidentiel 2015 décerné par Architectural Review. Il a également été lauréat du prix Perspective 40 under 40 Asia-Pacific Design Awards en architecture. Avant de rejoindre l'université de Hong Kong, où il est désormais professeur associé de pratique, Olivier était Unit Master à l'Architectural Association et a enseigné les studios de design à la Royal Academy de Copenhague ainsi qu'à l'EPFL en Suisse.

Olivier Ottevaere es arquitecto y profesor cuyo interés por la arquitectura se basa en un enfoque híbrido entre los experimentos físicos y las organizaciones geométricas. Sus proyectos se sustentan sobre tres líneas de interés la integración de los principios estructurales activos, las propiedades de los materiales y los procedimientos de construcción.

Trabajó en firmas de arquitectura en Nueva York, Lisboa y Londres hasta co fundar el estudio Double (o) en 2012. Su trabajo de investigación sobre prefabricados «House me tender», recibió el premio al Best Residential Future 2015 deArchitectural Review. También fue galardonado con los premios Perspective 40 under 40 Asia-Pacific de diseño en Arquitectura. Antes de incorporarse a la Universidad de Hong Kong donde ahora es profesor asociado de práctica, Olivier fue maestro de unidad en la Architectural Association y ha enseñado estudios de diseño en la Royal Academy de Copenhague, así como en la EPFL de Suiza.

DOUBLE (O)

OLIVIER OTTEVAERE

HONG KONG
WWW.DOUBLEOSTUDIO.COM

CASA TREVO

LISBON, PORTUGAL

Photos © Fabio Cunha, Marco Antunes

"Casa Trevo" or "Clover House", is a two-storey residence located south of Lisbon, Portugal. The project is located near the Atlantic Ocean, in a pine forest that rises above a sandy terrain.

The rooms are organised around three circular outdoor courtyards that function as extensions of the interior spaces, bringing light into the rooms through large openings.

The 9 m high courtyards also act as structural voids in the form of three hollow, half-open columns. Together, they support a series of floor slabs rising to different heights. They also support a water beam, which serves as a rooftop pool, the lower part of which presses into the spaces below.

The structure is made of concrete and plays with the ambiguity of mass and void, inside and outside. The house conveys autonomy and monumentality, despite its small size.

Thanks to its structure, the house produces its own introverted world facing the sun, with private yet mutable spaces that are intermittently revealed by the unabashed light of Lisbon.

„Casa Trevo" oder „Klee Haus" ist ein zweistöckiges Wohnhaus im Süden von Lissabon, Portugal. Das Projekt befindet sich in der Nähe des Atlantiks in einem Kiefernwald, der sich über sandiges Gelände erhebt.

Die Räume sind um drei kreisförmige Außenhöfe angeordnet, die als Erweiterung der Innenräume fungieren und durch große Öffnungen Licht in die Räume bringen.

Die neun Meter hohen Höfe fungieren auch als strukturelle Hohlräume in Form von drei hohlen, halboffenen Säulen. Gemeinsam tragen sie eine Reihe von Bodenplatten, die unterschiedlich hoch sind. Sie tragen auch einen Wasserbalken, der als Dachpool dient, dessen unterer Teil sich in die darunter liegenden Räume drückt.

Die Struktur besteht aus Ortbeton und spielt mit der Ambiguität von Masse und Leere, Innen und Außen. Das Haus strahlt trotz seiner geringen Größe Autonomie und Monumentalität aus.

Dank seiner Struktur schafft das Haus eine eigene, der Sonne zugewandte, introvertierte Welt mit privaten, aber wandelbaren Räumen, die von Zeit zu Zeit durch das unverschämte Licht Lissabons enthüllt werden.

« Casa Trevo » ou « Maison Trèfle », est une résidence de deux étages située au sud de Lisbonne, au Portugal. Le projet est situé près de l'océan Atlantique, dans une forêt de pins qui s'élève au-dessus d'un terrain sablonneux.

Les pièces sont organisées autour de trois cours extérieures circulaires qui fonctionnent comme des extensions des espaces intérieurs, apportant la lumière dans les pièces par de grandes ouvertures.

Les cours de neuf mètres de haut font également office de vides structurels sous la forme de trois colonnes creuses semi-ouvertes. Ensemble, ils soutiennent une série de dalles de plancher s'élevant à différentes hauteurs. Ils soutiennent également une poutre d'eau, qui sert de piscine sur le toit, dont la partie inférieure s'enfonce dans les espaces situés en dessous.

La structure est faite de béton in situ et joue avec l'ambiguïté de la masse et du vide, de l'intérieur et de l'extérieur. La maison dégage une autonomie et une monumentalité, malgré sa petite taille.

Grâce à sa structure, la maison produit son propre monde introverti face au soleil, avec des espaces privés mais mutables qui sont révélés par intermittence par la lumière sans retenue de Lisbonne.

La «Casa Trevo» o «Casa Trébol», es una residencia de dos plantas situada al sur de Lisboa, Portugal. El proyecto se encuentra cerca del Océano Atlántico, en un bosque de pinos que se eleva sobre un terreno arenoso.

Las habitaciones se organizan en torno a tres patios exteriores de forma circular que funcionan como extensiones de los ambientes interiores, y llevan la luz a las estancias a través de grandes aperturas.

Los patios, de nueve metros de altura, también actúan como vacíos estructurales en forma de tres columnas huecas y semi abiertas. En conjunto, soportan una serie de forjados que ascienden a diferentes alturas. También sostienen una viga de agua, que sirve de piscina en la azotea y cuya parte inferior presiona los espacios de abajo.

La estructura está hecha de hormigón in situ y juega con la ambigüedad de la masa y el vacío, del interior y el exterior. La casa transmite autonomía y monumentalidad, a pesar de su pequeño tamaño.

Gracias a su estructura, la vivienda produce su propio mundo introvertido de cara al sol, con espacios privados y a la vez mutables que se dejan ver de forma intermitente por la luz descarada de Lisboa.

Longitudinal section

1. Swimming pool   5. Bathroom
2. Bedroom 1   6. Dining room
3. Stairs   7. Atrium
4. Bedroom 2   8. Kitchen

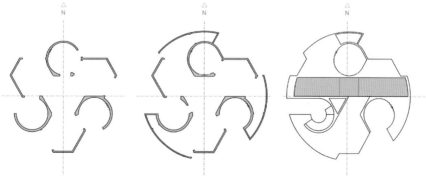

Ground floor plan   First floor plan   Roof top plan

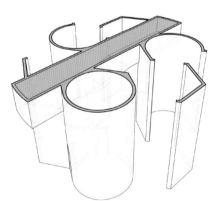

Primary structure

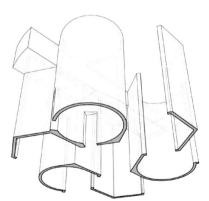

Architect: **Olivier Ottevaere & Elsa Caetano**
Local architect: **Marco Antunes**
Structural Engineer: **Joao Silva**
Contractor: **CS Construtora**

Gkotsis Serafimidou Architects was founded by Christos Gkotsis and Elena Serafimidou. Both have studied architecture at the University of Westminster in London and postgraduate studies at Columbia University in New York. The office is based in Athens and has projects both in Greece and abroad. Its work includes a wide range of typologies and scales, such as private residences, offices, professional offices and restaurants. The firm's projects search for the essence and its values, to create a lasting relationship between architecture, interior design and objects. Building integrity, persistence in detail and ergonomics play a key role in their design process and work.
The studio's creators are strong advocates of a strictly simple architectural language that communicates and explores modern aesthetics, but resists fashion and trends.

Gkotsis Serafimidou Architects wurde von Christos Gkotsis und Elena Serafimidou gegründet. Beide haben Architektur an der University of Westminster in London und ein Aufbaustudium an der Columbia University in New York absolviert. Das Büro hat seinen Sitz in Athen und führt Projekte sowohl in Griechenland als auch im Ausland durch. Ihre Arbeit umfasst ein breites Spektrum an Typologien und Maßstäben, wie z. B. Privatwohnungen, Büros, professionelle Büros und Restaurants. Die Projekte des Büros suchen nach dem Wesentlichen und seinen Werten, um eine dauerhafte Beziehung zwischen Architektur, Innenarchitektur und Objekten zu schaffen. Bauliche Integrität, Beharrlichkeit im Detail und Ergonomie spielen eine Schlüsselrolle in ihrem Entwurfsprozess und bei der Realisierung der Arbeiten.
Die Schöpfer des Studios sind überzeugte Verfechter einer strikt einfachen architektonischen Sprache, die eine moderne Ästhetik vermittelt und erforscht, sich aber Moden und Trends widersetzt.

Gkotsis Serafimidou Architects a été fondé par Christos Gkotsis et Elena Serafimidou. Tous deux ont étudié l'architecture à l'université de Westminster à Londres et ont suivi des études de troisième cycle à l'université Columbia à New York. Le bureau est basé à Athènes et a des projets tant en Grèce qu'à l'étranger. Son travail comprend un large éventail de typologies et d'échelles, telles que des résidences privées, des bureaux, des bureaux professionnels et des restaurants. Les projets du cabinet sont à la recherche de l'essence et de ses valeurs, afin de créer une relation durable entre l'architecture, l'aménagement intérieur et les objets. L'intégrité du bâtiment, la persistance dans le détail et l'ergonomie jouent un rôle clé dans leur processus de conception et la réalisation de l'œuvre.
Les créateurs du studio sont de fervents défenseurs d'un langage architectural strictement simple qui communique et explore l'esthétique moderne, mais résiste aux modes et aux tendances.

Gkotsis Serafimidou Architects fue fundado por Christos Gkotsis y Elena Serafimidou. Ambos han cursado estudios de arquitectura en la Universidad de Westminster de Londres y estudios de postgrado en la Universidad de Columbia de Nueva York. El despacho está situado en Atenas y cuenta con proyectos tanto en Grecia como en el extranjero. Su trabajo incluye un amplio abanico de tipologías y escalas, como residencias privadas, oficinas, despachos profesionales y restauración. Los proyectos de la firma buscan la esencia y sus valores, para crear una relación duradera entre la arquitectura, el diseño de interiores y los objetos. La integridad del edificio, la persistencia en el detalle y la ergonomía juegan un papel clave en su proceso de diseño y la realización de la obra.
Los creadores del estudio son firmes defensores del lenguaje arquitectónico estrictamente simple, que comunica y explora la estética moderna, pero se resiste a la moda y las tendencias.

GKOTSIS SERAFIMIDOU ARCHITECTS

CHRISTOS GKOTSIS, ELENA SERAFIMIDOU

ATHENS, GREECE
WWW.GASAP.GR

HOUSE IN MARMARI

EVIA, GREECE

Photos © George Messaritakis

This house, situated on a rocky, steeply sloping site overlooking the Petalioi islands, is the reconstruction of an existing building. The original structure has been respected for the renovation. The wooden ceilings and grouting were kept, but the openings were modified.

Due to the interior character of the previous building, the architects decided to use it for private areas such as bedrooms and bathrooms. At the same time they designed a white cube, which "lands" in the landscape and hovers in equilibrium at the steepest point of the site.

The cube houses the daytime functions with living, dining and kitchen areas in a single space with three large openings. The windows are arranged with respect to the views of the sea, the mountains and the harbour.

The main entrance and the connection between the old building and the new one takes place through a link: a glass and metal collar with perforations. The existing landscape remains largely intact, with the only intervention being the low stone walls, which create internal pathways and act as the main circulation system.

Dieses Haus, das auf einem felsigen, steil abfallenden Gelände mit Blick auf die Petalioi-Inseln liegt, ist der Wiederaufbau eines bestehenden Gebäudes. Bei der Renovierung wurde die ursprüngliche Struktur beibehalten. Die Holzdecken und Fugen wurden beibehalten, aber die Öffnungen wurden verändert.

Aufgrund des inneren Charakters des Vorgängerbaus entschieden sich die Architekten, diesen für private Bereiche wie Schlafzimmer und Bäder zu nutzen. Gleichzeitig entwarfen sie einen weißen Kubus, der in der Landschaft „landet" und an der steilsten Stelle des Geländes im Gleichgewicht schwebt.

Der Kubus beherbergt die Tagesfunktionen mit Wohn-, Ess- und Küchenbereich in einem einzigen Raum mit drei großen Öffnungen. Die Fenster sind so angeordnet, dass sie den Blick auf das Meer, die Berge und vor allem auf den Hafen freigeben.

Der Haupteingang und die Verbindung zwischen dem alten und dem neuen Gebäude erfolgt über ein Bindeglied: eine Glas- und Metallmanschette mit Perforationen. Die bestehende Landschaft bleibt weitgehend intakt, der einzige Eingriff sind die niedrigen Steinmauern, die die internen Wege bilden und als Hauptzirkulationssystem dienen.

Cette maison, située sur un site rocheux et en forte pente surplombant les îles Petalioi, est la reconstruction d'un bâtiment existant. La structure originale a été respectée pour la rénovation. Les plafonds et les joints en bois ont été conservés, mais les ouvertures ont été modifiées.

En raison du caractère intérieur du bâtiment précédent, les architectes ont décidé de l'utiliser pour les espaces privés tels que les chambres et les salles de bain. Parallèlement, ils ont conçu un cube blanc, qui « atterrit » dans le paysage et plane en équilibre au point le plus abrupt du site.

Le cube abrite les fonctions de jour avec les espaces de vie, de repas et de cuisine dans un seul espace doté de trois grandes ouvertures. Les fenêtres sont disposées en fonction de la vue sur la mer, les montagnes et, surtout, le port.

L'entrée principale et la connexion entre l'ancien bâtiment et le nouveau se fait par un lien : un collier de verre et de métal avec des perforations. Le paysage existant reste en grande partie intact, la seule intervention étant les murets de pierre, qui créent des voies internes et servent de système de circulation principal.

Esta casa situada en un terreno rocoso y muy inclinado con vistas a las islas Petalioi, es la reconstrucción de un edificio ya existente. Para la rehabilitación se ha respetado la estructura original. Se mantuvieron los techos de madera y la lechada, pero se modificaron las aberturas.

Debido al carácter de interioridad de la construcción previa, los arquitectos decidieron destinarlo a las zonas privadas como los dormitorios y los baños. Paralelamente diseñaron un cubo blanco, que «aterriza» en el paisaje y se mantiene flotando en equilibrio en el punto más escarpado del solar.

El cubo alberga las funciones diurnas con zonas de estar, comedor y cocina, en un único espacio con tres grandes aberturas. Los ventanales están dispuestos con respecto a las vistas al mar, la montaña y, con más énfasis, hacia el puerto.

El acceso principal y la conexión entre el edificio antiguo y el nuevo tienen lugar a través de un enlace: un cuello de vidrio y metal con perforaciones. El paisaje existente permanece, en su mayor parte, intacto, con la única intervención de los muros bajos de piedra, que crean caminos internos y actúan como sistema de circulación principal.

Hindley & Co's work is defined by its distilled simplicity; materials, textures, framed views, scale and light are carefully considered to create elegant, striking and highly functional homes.

Architect Anne Hindley, the studio's founder, worked for over twenty years for acclaimed international and local architects. In New York she began her career with Smith-Miller & Hawkinson, SITE and Gaetano Pesce. She was engaged by Daryl Jackson (Australia) and Bligh Voller Nield for the Etihad Stadium, and then returned overseas to embark on projects such as the redevelopment of the iconic Battersea Power Station in London, a grand home in Singapore, and an apartment building in Marseille. Back home in Melbourne, she became a senior architect at Allan Powell's Architecture studio where she honed her specialisation in beautifully detailed high end private houses.

Die Arbeit von Hindley & Co zeichnet sich durch ihre klare Einfachheit aus: Materialien, Texturen, Ausblicke, Größe und Licht werden sorgfältig berücksichtigt, um elegante, auffällige und hochfunktionale Häuser zu schaffen.

Die Architektin Anne Hindley, die Gründerin des Studios, hat über zwanzig Jahre lang für renommierte internationale und lokale Architekten gearbeitet. In New York begann sie ihre Karriere bei Smith-Miller & Hawkinson, SITE und Gaetano Pesce. Sie wurde von Daryl Jackson (Australien) und Bligh Voller Nield für das Etihad-Stadion engagiert und kehrte dann nach Übersee zurück, um an Projekten wie der Umgestaltung der ikonischen Battersea Power Station in London, ein großes Haus in Singapur und ein Apartmenthaus in Marseille. Zurück in Melbourne wurde sie leitende Architektin im Architekturbüro Allan Powell's Architecture, wo sie ihr Spezialgebiet, die detailreichen und hochwertigen Privathäuser, verfeinerte.

Le travail de Hindley & Co se définit par sa simplicité distillée ; les matériaux, les textures, les vues encadrées, l'échelle et la lumière sont soigneusement étudiés pour créer des maisons élégantes, frappantes et hautement fonctionnelles. L'architecte Anne Hindley, fondatrice du studio, a travaillé pendant plus de vingt ans pour des architectes locaux et internationaux de renom. À New York, elle a commencé sa carrière chez Smith-Miller & Hawkinson, SITE et Gaetano Pesce. Elle a été engagée par Daryl Jackson (Australie) et Bligh Voller Nield pour l'Etihad Stadium, puis est retournée à l'étranger pour se lancer dans des projets tels que le réaménagement de l'emblématique Battersea Power Station à Londres, une grande maison à Singapour et un immeuble d'appartements à Marseille. De retour à Melbourne, elle est devenue architecte senior au studio d'architecture d'Allan Powell, où elle a affiné son domaine de spécialisation dans les maisons privées haut de gamme magnifiquement détaillées.

El trabajo de Hindley & Co se define por su destilada simplicidad; los materiales, las texturas, las vistas enmarcadas, la escala y la luz son cuidadosamente considerados para crear hogares elegantes, llamativos y altamente funcionales. La arquitecta Anne Hindley, fundadora del estudio, trabajó más de veinte años para aclamados arquitectos internacionales y locales. En Nueva York comenzó su carrera con Smith-Miller & Hawkinson, SITE y Gaetano Pesce. Fue contratada por Daryl Jackson (Australia) y Bligh Voller Nield para el Etihad Stadium, y luego volvió al extranjero para embarcarse en proyectos como la remodelación de la emblemática Battersea Power Station en Londres, una vivienda en Singapur y un edificio de apartamentos en Marsella. De vuelta a casa en Melbourne, fue arquitecta principal en el estudio del arquitecto Allan Powell, donde perfeccionó su especialización en residencias privadas de alto nivel con gran cantidad de detalles.

HINDLEY & CO

ANNE HINDLEY

MELBOURNE, AUSTRALIA
WWW.HINDLEYANDCO.COM.AU

THE SANCTUARY OF THE DUNES

VICTORIA, AUSTRALIA

Photos © Tatjana Plitt

The home is a renovation of a 1960s beach shack nestled among the dunes of Diamond Bay. Its owners, a family with a special design sensibility, came to the architects with an image of the pronounced veranda of Mies Van der Rohe's Farnsworth House, which, together with the qualities of the site, was the starting point for the project. The house has two levels. Access to the upper level is via a sculptural ramp where the master bedroom and communal areas are located. The lower level houses the children's rooms, guest, play and service areas. The style had to be timeless, and to this end, modernist design from the 1930s and 1950s and high quality materials were employed. The travertine cladding, windows and structure in pale, natural colours match the local Sorrento limestone and blend harmoniously with the surrounding dunes and trees. Due to the integrated nature of the architecture and interior design, few but very well selected pieces of designer furniture were used. The minimalist character helped to create a new type of beach house, sophisticated and relaxed at the same time.

Bei dem Haus handelt es sich um die renovierung einer strandhütte aus den 1960er jahren, die in den Dünen der Diamond Bay liegt. Die Besitzer, eine Familie mit einem besonderen Sinn für Design, kamen zu den Architekten mit einem bild der ausgeprägten Veranda von Mies Van der Rohe Farnsworth House, das zusammen mit den qualitäten des ortes den ausgangspunkt für das projekt bildete. Das Haus hat zwei ebenen. Der zugang zur oberen ebene erfolgt über eine skulpturale rampe, auf der sich das Hauptschlafzimmer und die gemeinschaftsräume befinden. Die untere ebene beherbergt die kinderzimmer, gäste-, spiel- und servicebereiche. Der Stil sollte zeitlos sein, und zu diesem Zweck wurden modernistisches design aus den 1930er und 1950er jahren und hochwertige materialien verwendet. Die travertinverkleidung, die fenster und die struktur in hellen, natürlichen farben passen zum lokalen Sorrentiner kalkstein und fügen sich harmonisch in die umliegenden dünen und bäume ein. Aufgrund des integrierten charakters der architektur und der Inneneinrichtung wurden nur wenige, aber sehr gut ausgewählte designermöbel verwendet. Der minimalistische charakter trug dazu bei, einen neuen typus von strandhaus zu schaffen, der gleichzeitig anspruchsvoll und entspannt ist.

La maison est une rénovation d'une cabane de plage des années 1960 nichée parmi les dunes de Diamond Bay. Ses propriétaires, une famille dotée d'une sensibilité particulière en matière de design, sont venus voir les architectes avec une image de la véranda prononcée de la maison Farnsworth de Mies Van der Rohe, qui, avec les qualités du site, a été le point de départ du projet. La maison comporte deux niveaux. L'accès au niveau supérieur se fait par une rampe sculpturale où se trouvent la chambre principale et les espaces communs. Le niveau inférieur abrite les chambres des enfants, les espaces réservés aux invités, aux jeux et aux services. Le style devait être intemporel et, à cette fin, un design moderniste des années 1930 et 1950 et des matériaux de haute qualité ont été utilisés. Le revêtement en travertin, les fenêtres et la structure aux couleurs pâles et naturelles s'harmonisent avec la pierre calcaire locale de Sorrento et se fondent harmonieusement avec les dunes et les arbres environnants. En raison de la nature intégrée de l'architecture et de la décoration intérieure, peu de meubles de designers ont été utilisés, mais ils ont été très bien choisis. Le caractère minimaliste a permis de créer un nouveau type de maison de plage, à la fois sophistiquée et détendue.

La vivienda es una renovación de una cabaña de playa de los años sesenta situada entre las dunas de Diamond Bay. Sus propietarios, una familia con especial sensibilidad para el diseño, acudieron a los arquitectos con una imagen de la pronunciada veranda de la Casa Farnsworth, de Mies Van der Rohe, que, junto con las cualidades del emplazamiento, fue el punto de partida del proyecto. La casa tiene dos niveles. El acceso a la planta superior se realiza a través de una rampa escultórica donde se encuentra el dormitorio principal y las zonas de uso común. El nivel inferior aloja las habitaciones de los hijos, zona de invitados, de juegos y de servicios El estilo debía ser atemporal y para ello se recurrió al diseño modernista de los años 30 y 50 y los materiales de alta calidad. El revestimiento de travertino, las ventanas y la estructura de colores pálidos y naturales se ajustan a la piedra caliza local de Sorrento y se funden armoniosamente con las dunas y los árboles del entorno. Debido a la naturaleza integrada de la arquitectura y el diseño interior, se pusieron pocas pero muy bien seleccionadas piezas de mobiliario de diseño. El carácter minimalista contribuyó a crear un nuevo tipo de casa de playa, sofisticada y relajada a la vez.

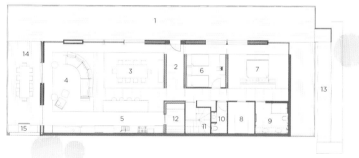

Upper floor

1. Veranda   8. Wir
2. Entry   9. Ensuite
3. Dining   10. Powder
4. Family room   11. Stair
5. Kitchen   12. Pantry
6. Bedroom   13. Ramp
7. Master   14. Alfresco
   bedroom   15. Bbq

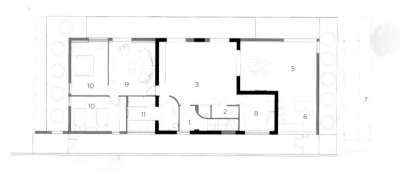

Lower floor

1. Hall   7. Ramp
2. Store   8. Laundry
3. Games room   9. Guest living
4. Laundry   10. Bedroom
5. Man cave   11. Bathroom
6. Bar

Sand Dune Sanctuary kitchen and living room

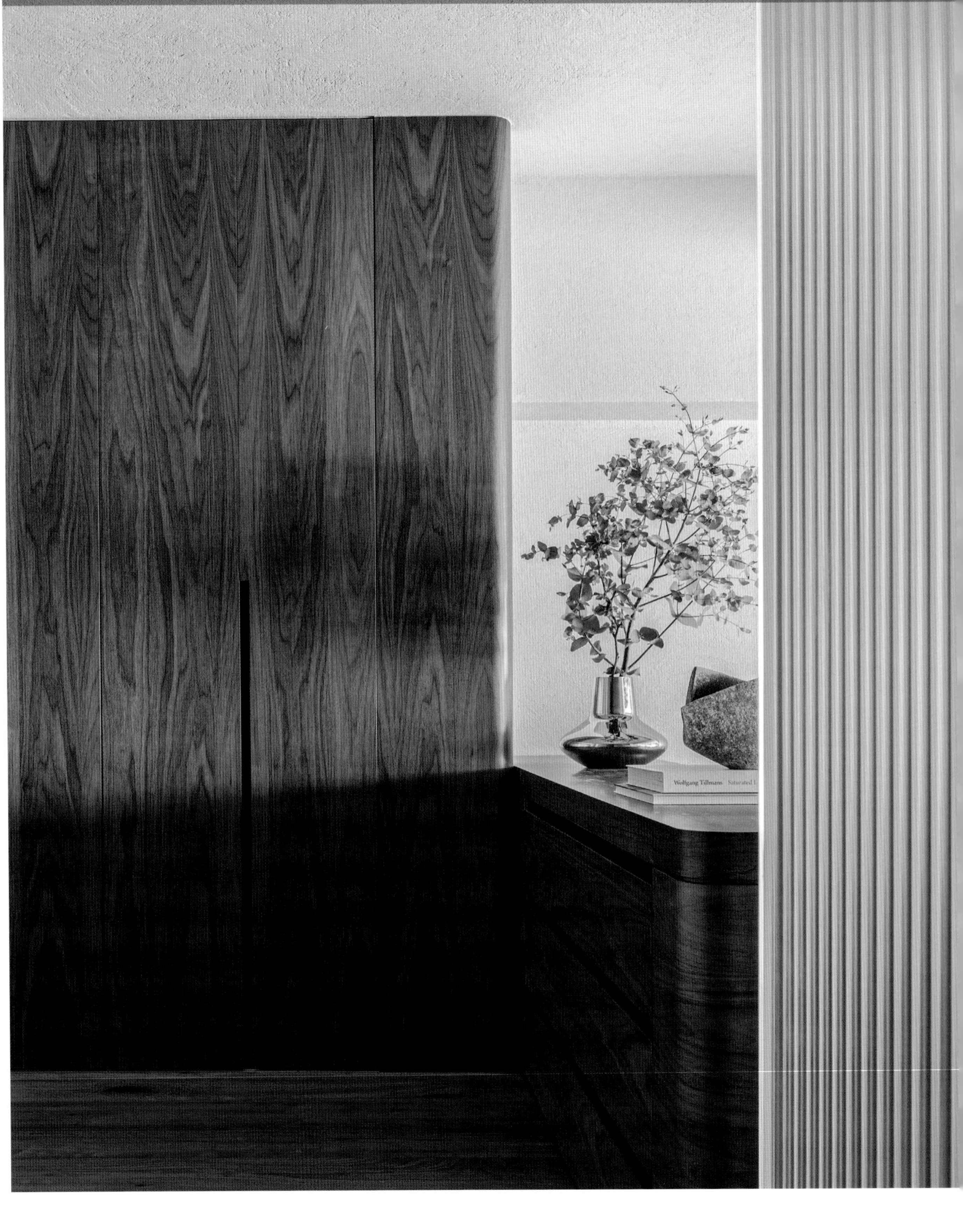
Wolfgang Tillmans

I IN Inc. is a Tokyo-based design studio founded in 2018 by Yohei Terui and Hiromu Yuyama. The firm is focused on finding innovative solutions in space design, and proposes striking and surprising interiors.
Yohei graduated in interior design from Parsons School of Design in New York in 2008, after attending Meiji University in Tokyo. Between 2009 and 2017, he worked at Curiosity, where he was a senior designer, and before that he worked at New York-based Gabellini Sheppard and SHoP Architects.
Hiromu studied architecture and interior design at ICS College of Arts and graduated from Gakugei University in Tokyo. He also worked at Curiosity as a senior designer on several global projects. Previously, he worked at ILYA in Tokyo.

I IN Inc. ist ein Designstudio mit Sitz in Tokio, das 2018 von Yohei Terui und Hiromu Yuyama gegründet wurde. Das Unternehmen konzentriert sich auf die Suche nach innovativen Lösungen für die Raumgestaltung und schlägt auffallende und überraschende Innenräume vor.
Yohei schloss 2008 sein Studium der Innenarchitektur an der Parsons School of Design in New York ab, nachdem er die Meiji University in Tokio besucht hatte. Zwischen 2009 und 2017 arbeitete er bei Curiosity, wo er als Senior Designer tätig war. Davor arbeitete er bei Gabellini Sheppard und SHoP Architects in New York.
Hiromu studierte Architektur und Innenarchitektur am ICS College of Arts und machte seinen Abschluss an der Gakugei-Universität in Tokio. Er arbeitete auch bei Curiosity als Senior Designer an mehreren globalen Projekten und war zuvor bei ILYA in Tokio tätig.

I IN Inc. est un studio de design basé à Tokyo, fondé en 2018 par Yohei Terui et Hiromu Yuyama. Le cabinet s'attache à trouver des solutions innovantes en matière d'aménagement de l'espace, et propose des intérieurs saisissants et surprenants.
Yohei est diplômé en design d'intérieur de la Parsons School of Design de New York en 2008, après avoir fréquenté l'université Meiji de Tokyo. Entre 2009 et 2017, il a travaillé chez Curiosity, où il était designer senior, et avant cela, il a travaillé chez Gabellini Sheppard et SHoP Architects, basés à New York.
Hiromu a étudié l'architecture et la décoration d'intérieur à l'ICS College of Arts et est diplômé de l'université Gakugei de Tokyo. Il a également travaillé chez Curiosity en tant que concepteur principal sur plusieurs projets mondiaux. Auparavant, il a travaillé chez ILYA à Tokyo.

I IN Inc. es un estudio de diseño con sede en Tokio fundado en 2018 por Yohei Terui y Hiromu Yuyama. La firma está enfocada en la búsqueda de soluciones innovadoras en el diseño de espacios, y propone interiores impactantes y sorprendentes.
Yohei se licenció en diseño de interiores en la Parsons School of Design de Nueva York en 2008, tras pasar por la Universidad Meiji de Tokio. Entre 2009 y 2017, trabajó en Curiosity, donde se desempeñó como diseñador principal y antes trabajó en las empresas neoyorquinas Gabellini Sheppard y SHoP Architects.
Hiromu por su parte, estudió arquitectura y diseño de interiores en el ICS College of Arts. También se graduó en la Universidad Gakugei de Tokio. También trabajó en Curiosity como diseñador principal en varios proyectos globales anteriormente, trabajó en ILYA en Tokio.

I IN

HIROMU YUYAMA, YOHEI TERUI

TOKYO, JAPAN
WWW.I-IN.JP

THELIFE SUITENGUMAE

TOKYO, JAPAN

Photos © Tomooki Kengaku

This show flat for the new THELIFE line of Smarg real estate offers an innovative take on the world of refurbishment. I IN took care of the branding, from the interior design to the brand name, logo and scent. The aim was to revive the living space of the existing condominiums, with a configuration of fluid environments adapted to modern living. To this end, the designers set out to achieve the necessary communion between clarity and space. The bathroom partition, made of corrugated glass, lets in light with a unique effect while dividing the scene. On the other hand, the division of the bedroom and living room with storage furniture enhances the feeling of unity and spaciousness. The edges of the wooden walls are curved, a detail that has always been very present in Japan and brings the idea of familiarity. Their texture and soft sheen are reminiscent of the cylindrical pillars of Japanese architecture. The plaster finish captures the ever-changing light, and provides a comfortable flow of time in all rooms. Although it is a modern space, the minimalist configuration results in a dwelling that the user can connect with for a long time.

Diese Musterwohnung für die neue THELIFE-Linie der Smarg-Immobilien bietet eine innovative Sichtweise auf die Welt der Renovierung. I IN kümmerte sich um das Branding, von der Inneneinrichtung bis zum Markennamen, dem Logo und dem Duft. Ziel war es, den Lebensraum der bestehenden Eigentumswohnungen mit einer an das moderne Leben angepassten Konfiguration von fließenden Umgebungen neu zu beleben. Zu diesem Zweck haben sich die Designer bemüht, die notwendige Verbindung zwischen Klarheit und Raum herzustellen. Die Badezimmerabtrennung aus gewelltem Glas lässt das Licht mit einem einzigartigen Effekt eindringen und unterteilt die Szene. Die Trennung von Schlaf- und Wohnzimmer mit Stauraummöbeln verstärkt hingegen das Gefühl von Einheitlichkeit und Geräumigkeit. Die Kanten der Holzwände sind geschwungen, ein Detail, das in Japan schon immer sehr präsent war und den Eindruck von Vertrautheit vermittelt. Ihre Textur und ihr weicher Glanz erinnern an die zylindrischen Säulen der japanischen Architektur.Die Putzoberfläche fängt das ständig wechselnde Licht ein und sorgt für einen angenehmen Zeitfluss in allen Räumen. Obwohl es sich um einen modernen Raum handelt, führt die minimalistische Gestaltung zu einer Wohnung, mit der sich der Benutzer lange Zeit identifizieren kann.

Cet appartement témoin de la nouvelle gamme de biens immobiliers Smarg THELIFE offre une vision innovante du monde de la rénovation. Je me suis occupé de l'image de marque, de la décoration intérieure au nom de la marque, au logo et au parfum. L'objectif était de faire revivre l'espace de vie des condominiums existants, avec une configuration d'environnements fluides adaptés à la vie moderne. À cette fin, les concepteurs ont cherché à réaliser la communion nécessaire entre la clarté et l'espace.
La cloison de la salle de bains, réalisée en verre ondulé, laisse entrer la lumière avec un effet unique tout en divisant la scène. D'autre part, la division de la chambre à coucher et du salon par des meubles de rangement renforce le sentiment d'unité et d'espace. Les bords des murs en bois sont incurvés, un détail qui a toujours été très présent au Japon et qui apporte l'idée de familiarité. Leur texture et leur brillance douce rappellent les piliers cylindriques de l'architecture japonaise.La finition en plâtre capture la lumière toujours changeante, et permet une circulation confortable du temps dans toutes les pièces. Bien qu'il s'agisse d'un espace moderne, la configuration minimaliste donne lieu à un logement avec lequel l'utilisateur peut se connecter pendant longtemps.

Este piso de muestra para la nueva línea de THELIFE de la inmobiliaria Smarg, propone una visión innovadora sobre el mundo de las reformas. I IN se hizo cargo del branding, desde el diseño del interiorismo hasta el nombre de la marca, el logotipo y el aroma. El objetivo era hacer renacer el espacio vital de los condominios existentes, con una configuración de ambientes fluidos adaptados a la vida moderna. Para ello los diseñadores se plantean unos recursos para la necesaria comunión entre la claridad y el espacio.
El tabique del cuarto de baño, hecho de vidrio ondulado, deja pasar la luz con un efecto único, a la vez que divide la escena. Por otra parte, la división del dormitorio y la sala de estar a partir de muebles de almacenaje, aumenta la sensación de unidad y amplitud. Los cantos de las paredes de madera están curvados, un detalle que ha estado siempre muy presente en Japón y que aporta la idea de familiaridad. Su textura y suave brillo, recuerda a los pilares cilíndricos de la arquitectura de ese país.El acabado de yeso capta la luz siempre cambiante, y proporciona un cómodo flujo del tiempo en todos los ambientes. Aunque se trata de un espacio moderno, la configuración minimalista da lugar a una vivienda con la que el usuario puede conectar durante mucho tiempo.

MASTERMIND OFFICES

TOKYO, JAPAN

Photos © Norihito Yamauchi

The spirit of a Japanese fashion brand has been imprinted in the remodelling of its offices in the city of Tokyo. True to the minimalist aesthetic of the high-end streetwear brand, I IN created a design with minimal elements emphasised by colour and light.
The brand, well known for its iconic skull logo, needed two distinct areas in its premises: one for work and one for presentations.
Black and white are the colours linked to the brand's identity. The designers therefore opted for a monochromatic scheme and luxurious materials to create a juxtaposition between the two floors with identical layouts: one in white and the other in black.
The lighting design was a key element in creating a unique ambience for each level. The white floor uses office-like lighting, while the black space has light box ceiling lamps that contrast with the dark interior. The white space reflects the soft shadows created by the light, and the black lines provide a pleasant accent.

Der Geist einer japanischen Modemarke hat sich bei der Umgestaltung ihrer Büros in der Stadt Tokio nie- dergeschlagen. Getreu der minimalistischen Ästhetik der High-End- Streetwear-Marke entwarf I IN ein Design mit minimalen Elementen, die durch Farbe und Licht betont werden.
Die Marke, die für ihr ikonisches Totenkopf-Logo bekannt ist, benötigte zwei verschiedene Bereiche in ihren Räumlichkeiten: einen für die Arbeit und einen für Präsentationen.
Schwarz und Weiß sind die Farben, die mit der Identität der Marke verbunden sind. Die Designer entschieden sich daher für ein monochromes Schema und luxuriöse Materialien, um eine Gegenüberstellung der beiden identisch gestalteten Etagen zu schaffen: eine in Weiß und eine in Schwarz.
Das Lichtdesign war ein Schlüsselelement für die Schaffung eines einzigartigen Ambientes für jede Ebene. Der weiße Fußboden ist mit einer büroähnlichen Beleuchtung versehen, während der schwarze Raum mit hellen Deckenlampen ausgestattet ist, die einen Kontrast zum dunklen Interieur bilden. Der weiße Raum spiegelt die weichen Schatten wider, die das Licht erzeugt, und die schwarzen Linien setzen einen angenehmen Akzent.

L'esprit d'une marque de mode japonaise s'est imprimé dans le remodelage de ses bureaux dans la ville de Tokyo. Fidèle à l'esthétique minimaliste de la marque de streetwear de luxe, j'ai créé un de- sign aux éléments minimaux mis en valeur par la couleur et la lumière.
La marque, bien connue pour son logo iconique de la tête de mort, avait besoin de deux espaces distincts dans ses locaux : un pour le travail et un pour les présentations.
Le noir et le blanc sont les couleurs liées à l'identité de la marque. Les concepteurs ont donc opté pour un schéma monochrome et des matériaux luxueux afin de créer une juxtaposition entre les deux étages aux agencements identiques : l'un en blanc et l'autre en noir.
La conception de l'éclairage a été un élément clé pour créer une ambiance unique à chaque niveau. Le sol blanc utilise un éclairage de type bureau, tandis que l'espace noir est équipé de plafonniers à caissons lumineux qui contrastent avec l'intérieur sombre. L'espace blanc reflète les ombres douces créées par la lumière, et les lignes noires apportent un accent agréable.

El espíritu de una marca japonesa de moda, ha quedado impreso en la remodelación de sus oficinas en la ciudad de Tokio. Fiel a la estética minimalista de la firma de streetwear de alta gama, I IN creó un diseño con elementos mínimos enfatizados por el color y la luz.
La marca, muy conocida por el icónico logotipo de la calavera, necesitaba dos zonas diferenciadas en sus instalaciones: una para el trabajo y otra para las presentaciones.
El blanco y el negro son los colores vinculados a la identidad de la marca. Por ello, los diseñadores se decantaron por un esquema monocromático y materiales de lujo para crear una yuxtaposición entre las dos plantas de distribución idéntica: una en blanco y otra en negro.
El diseño de la iluminación ha sido un elemento clave a la hora de construir un ambiente único para cada nivel. La planta blanca recurre a una iluminación similar a la de una oficina, mientras que el espacio negro cuenta con lámparas en el techo techo tipo caja de luz que contrastan con el interior oscuro. El espacio blanco refleja las suaves sombras creadas por la luz, y las líneas negras aportan un agradable acento.

Iwetta Ullenboom is an interior and object designer. After graduating from architecture at the Technical University of Berlin, she started her career in the field of interior design, creating spatial concepts for museums and art exhibitions. She continued her creative career working in various international studios where she gathered extensive experience in projects for shops, offices, homes, restaurants and hotels. During this time she honed her own personal aesthetic and design skills. In 2018, she decided to follow her own paths and established her own studio. The identity of the work lies in serene spaces, always with an astute attention to detail and a timeless aesthetic. Her love for minimalism and honest materials such as wood, marble and natural fabrics are characteristic elements of her works. In 2021, she co-founded the design studio ōna, specialising in unique pieces of furniture and decorative objects.

Iwetta Ullenboom ist Innenarchitektin und Objektdesignerin. Nach ihrem Architekturstudium an der Technischen Universität Berlin begann sie ihre berufliche Laufbahn im Bereich der Innenarchitektur und entwarf Raumkonzepte für Museen und Kunstausstellungen. Sie setzte ihre kreative Karriere in verschiedenen internationalen Studios fort, wo sie umfangreiche Erfahrungen bei Projekten für Geschäfte, Büros, Wohnungen, Restaurants und Hotels sammelte. Während dieser Zeit verfeinerte sie ihre persönliche Ästhetik und ihre Designfähigkeiten. Im Jahr 2018 beschloss sie ihren eigenen Weg zu gehen und gründete ihr eigenes Studio. Die Identität ihrer Arbeit liegt in den ruhigen Räumen, die sie immer mit viel Liebe zum Detail und einer zeitlosen Ästhetik gestaltet. Ihre Vorliebe für Minimalismus und ehrliche Materialien wie Holz, Marmor und natürliche Stoffe sind charakteristische Elemente ihrer Werke. Im Jahr 2021 war sie Mitbegründerin des Designstudios ōna, das sich auf einzigartige Möbel und dekorative Objekte spezialisiert hat.

Iwetta Ullenboom est une designer d'intérieur et d'objets. Après avoir obtenu un diplôme d'architecture à l'université technique de Berlin, elle a commencé sa carrière dans le domaine de la décoration intérieure, en créant des concepts spatiaux pour des musées et des expositions d'art. Elle a poursuivi sa carrière créative en travaillant dans divers studios internationaux où elle a acquis une vaste expérience dans des projets de magasins, de bureaux, de maisons, de restaurants et d'hôtels. Pendant cette période, elle a affiné son esthétique personnelle et ses compétences en matière de design. En 2018, elle décide de suivre ses propres chemins et crée son propre studio. L'identité de son travail réside dans des espaces sereins, toujours avec une attention particulière aux détails et une esthétique intemporelle. Son amour pour le minimalisme et les matériaux honnêtes tels que le bois, le marbre et les tissus naturels sont des éléments caractéris- tiques de ses œuvres. En 2021, elle cofonde le studio de design ōna, spécialisé dans les pièces uniques de mobilier et les objets décoratifs.

Iwetta Ullenboom es una diseñadora de interiores y objetos. Tras licenciarse en arquitectura en la Universidad Técnica de Berlín, comenzó su carrera en el ámbito del diseño de interiores, creando conceptos espaciales para museos y exposiciones de arte. Continuó su trayectoria creativa trabajando en varios estudios internacionales en los que reunió una amplia experiencia en proyectos para tiendas, oficinas, viviendas, restaurantes y hoteles. Durante ese tiempo fue perfeccionando su propia estética personal y sus habilidades de diseño. En 2018, decidió seguir sus propios caminos y estableció su propio estudio. La identidad de su trabajo está en los espacios serenos, siempre con una astuta atención al detalle y una estética atemporal. Su amor por el minimalismo y los materiales honestos como la madera, el mármol y los tejidos naturales son elementos característicos de sus obras. En 2021, cofundó el estudio de diseño ōna, especializado en piezas de mobiliario y objetos de decoración únicos.

IWETTA ULLENBOOM

IWETTA ULLENBOOM

BERLIN, GERMANY
WWW.IWETTAULLENBOOM.COM

AZ18

BERLIN, GERMANY

Photos © Sebastian Mowka

With the prerogative of creating a modern and refined interior, this penthouse has been renovated and redesigned for a young family. It is located on the eighth floor of a modern apartment complex, overlooking the vibrant Friedrichstraße area of Berlin.

The open-plan layout of the living room allows natural light to enter from opposite sides, providing a feeling of spaciousness throughout the day. The centrepiece of the living room is a monumental piece of wooden furniture arranged as a central box, with an undulating front surface. This structure, which houses a fireplace and storage space, defines the open layout of the space, with a cosy sitting area at the front and a hidden office area at the back. The central position of the box allows circulation on all sides and conceals some structural elements of the building. The minimalist library on the opposite side of the room, constructed from the same dark oak, creates a counterpart to the central cupboard. A variety of high-quality materials, such as oak, brass and marble, coexist harmoniously with more informal textures such as wicker and wool.

Unter der Prämisse, ein modernes und raffiniertes Interieur zu schaffen, wurde dieses Penthouse für eine junge Familie renoviert und umgestaltet. Es befindet sich im achten Stock eines modernen Wohnkomplexes mit Blick auf die pulsierende Friedrichstraße in Berlin.

Der offene Grundriss des Wohnzimmers ermöglicht den Einfall von natürlichem Licht von den gegenüberliegenden Seiten und vermittelt den ganzen Tag über ein Gefühl von Großzügigkeit. Das Herz des Wohnzimmers bildet ein monumentales Holzmöbelstück in Form eines zentralen Kastens mit wellenförmiger Frontfläche. Diese Struktur, die einen Kamin und Stauraum beherbergt, definiert die offene Raumaufteilung mit einer gemütlichen Sitzecke im vorderen und einem versteckten Bürobereich im hinteren Bereich. Die zentrale Lage der Box ermöglicht die Zirkulation auf allen Seiten und verbirgt einige strukturelle Elemente des Gebäudes. Die minimalistische Bibliothek auf der gegenüberliegenden Seite des Raumes, die aus der gleichen dunklen Eiche gefertigt ist, bildet das Gegenstück zum zentralen Schrank. Hochwertige Materialien wie Eiche, Messing und Marmor stehen harmonisch neben informelleren Texturen wie Rattan und Wolle.

Sous la prérogative de créer un intérieur moderne et raffiné, ce penthouse a été rénové et réaménagé pour une jeune famille. Il est situé au huitième étage d'un complexe d'appartements moderne, donnant sur le quartier animé de Friedrichstraße à Berlin.

La disposition ouverte du salon permet à la lumière naturelle d'entrer par les côtés opposés, ce qui donne une sensation d'espace tout au long de la journée. La pièce maîtresse du salon est un meuble monumental en bois disposé comme une boîte centrale, avec une surface frontale ondulée. Cette structure, qui abrite une cheminée et un espace de rangement, définit la disposition ouverte de l'espace, avec un coin salon confortable à l'avant et un coin bureau caché à l'arrière. La position centrale de la boîte permet une circulation sur tous les côtés et dissimule certains éléments structurels du bâtiment. La bibliothèque minimaliste située de l'autre côté de la pièce, construite dans le même chêne foncé, fait pendant à l'armoire centrale. Une variété de matériaux de haute qualité, tels que le chêne, le laiton et le marbre, coexistent harmonieusement avec des textures plus informelles comme l'osier et la laine.

Bajo la prerrogativa de crear un interior moderno y refinado, este ático ha sido reformado y rediseñado para una joven familia. Está situado en la octava planta de un moderno complejo de apartamentos, con vistas a la vibrante zona de Friedrichstraße, en Berlín.

La disposición abierta de la sala de estar permite que la luz natural ingrese desde lados opuestos, lo que aporta una sensación de amplitud durante todo el día. La pieza central del salón es un monumental mueble de madera dispuesto como una caja central, con una superficie frontal ondulada. Esta estructura que alberga una chimenea y espacio de almacenamiento, define la disposición abierta del espacio, con una acogedora zona de estar en la parte delantera y una zona de despacho oculta en la parte trasera. La posición central de la caja permite la circulación por todos los laterales y oculta algunos elementos estructurales del edificio. La biblioteca minimalista situada en el lado opuesto de la sala y construida con el mismo roble oscuro, crea una contrapartida al armario central. Una variedad de materiales de alta calidad, como el roble, el latón y el mármol, conviven armoniosamente con texturas más informales como el mimbre y la lana.

Floor plan

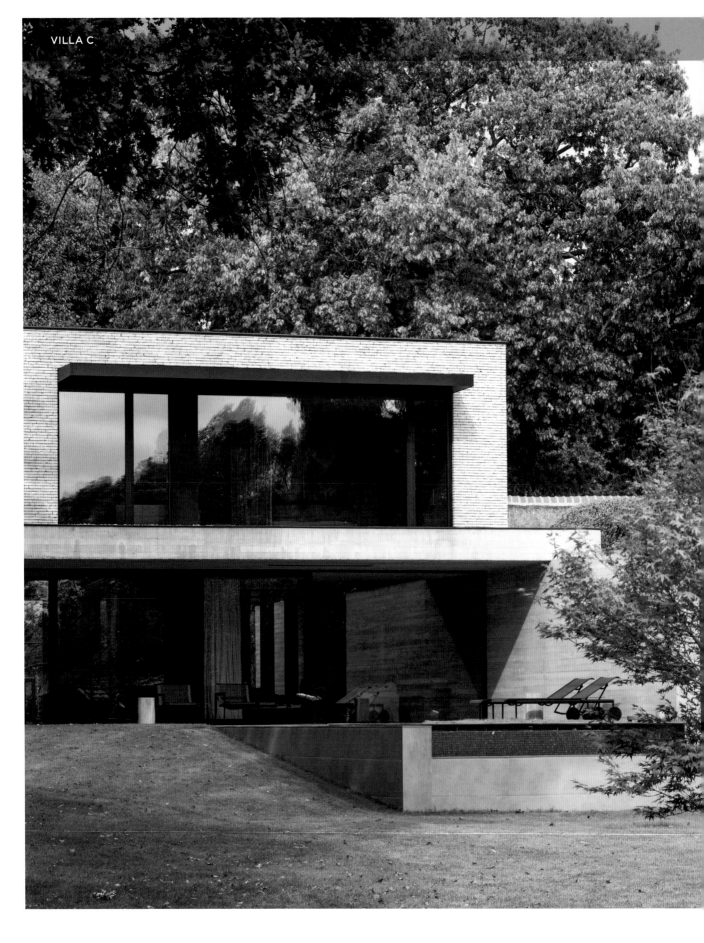

JUMA architects was founded by Mathieu Luyens and Julie van De Keere in 2009. Both architects, graduates of the Saint-Lucas Academy in Ghent, worked in studios in Antwerp and Ibiza before founding their own.

JUMA's work is determined by a modern, minimalist aesthetic, with careful use of light, space, emotion and the unique characteristics of each site. Throughout the creative process, their projects will incorporate different layers of detail. As a result, a spectrum of refined designs is generated, enhancing a quality result.

The firm's goal is to carry out a project efficiently, from the early planning stages to the detailing of materials and furniture design. Their specific approach allows them to be both passionate designers and functional builders in the creation of a cost-effective and personal structure.

JUMA architects wurde 2009 von Mathieu Luyens und Julie van De Keere gegründet. Beide Architekten, Absolventen der Saint-Lucas-Akademie in Gent, arbeiteten in Studios in Antwerpen und auf Ibiza, bevor sie ihr eigenes gründeten.

Die Arbeit von JUMA zeichnet sich durch eine moderne, minimalistische Ästhetik aus, bei der Licht, Raum, Emotionen und die einzigartigen Merkmale des jeweiligen Standorts sorgfältig genutzt werden. Während des gesamten kreativen Prozesses werden die Projekte verschiedene Ebenen von Details enthalten. So entsteht ein Spektrum an raffinierten Entwürfen, die zu einem hochwertigen Ergebnis führen.

Das Ziel der Firma ist es, ein Projekt von der ersten Planungsphase bis hin zu den Details der Materialien und des Möbeldesigns effizient durchzuführen. Ihr spezifischer Ansatz ermöglicht es ihnen, sowohl leidenschaftliche Designer als auch funktionale Bauherren bei der Schaffung einer kostengünstigen und persönlichen Struktur zu sein.

JUMA architects a été fondé par Mathieu Luyens et Julie van De Keere en 2009. Les deux architectes, diplômés de l'Académie Saint-Lucas de Gand, ont travaillé dans des studios à Anvers et à Ibiza avant de fonder leur propre studio.

Le travail de JUMA se caractérise par une esthétique moderne et minimaliste, avec une utilisation minutieuse de la lumière, de l'espace, de l'émotion et des caractéristiques uniques de chaque site. Tout au long du processus de création, leurs projets intégreront différentes couches de détails. Il en résulte un éventail de conceptions raffinées qui permettent d'obtenir un résultat de qualité.

L'objectif de l'entreprise est de mener à bien un projet de manière efficace, depuis les premières étapes de la planification jusqu'aux détails des matériaux et à la conception du mobilier. Leur approche spécifique leur permet d'être à la fois des concepteurs passionnés et des constructeurs fonctionnels dans la création d'une structure rentable et personnelle.

JUMA architects fue fundado por Mathieu Luyens y Julie van De Keere en 2009. Ambos arquitectos, egresados de la Saint-Lucas Academy de Gante, trabajaron en estudios de Amberes e Ibiza antes de fundar el suyo propio.

El trabajo de JUMA se caracteriza por una estética moderna y minimalista, con un uso cuidadoso de la luz, el espacio, la emoción y las características únicas de cada lugar. A lo largo del proceso de creación, sus proyectos incorporaran diferentes capas de detalle. Como resultado, se genera un espectro de diseños refinados que realzan un resultado de calidad.

El objetivo de la firma es llevar a cabo un proyecto de forma eficiente, desde las primeras fases de planificación hasta el detalle de los materiales y el diseño del mobiliario. Su enfoque específico les permite ser tanto diseñadores apasionados como constructores funcionales en la creación de una estructura rentable y personal.

JUMA ARCHITECTS

JULIE VAN DE KEERE, MATHIEU LUYENS

GHENT, BELGIUM
WWW.JUMAARCHITECTS.COM

VILLA C

SINT-MARTENS-LATEM, BELGIUM

Photos © Annick Vernimmen

For the design of this house, JUMA was asked to develop a compact floor plan suitable for everyday living. The result is a rather cubic volume, enlivened by a vivid play of contrasting materials.

As the house is set back from the street, the architects created a visual connection between the front and rear courtyard. To this end, a sturdy concrete wall runs along the front of the site. The wall continues through the interior of the house —along the corner of the desk and the living room— to finally end at the rear area, parallel to the swimming pool. Along this wall, large sections of glass accentuate the architectural image, creating transparency and open sight lines.

Inside, the finishes contribute to a sober, minimalist appearance. The cement and concrete walls contrast with the black wood that dominates the kitchen and dining room, and natural-coloured wood in the bedrooms and washrooms. The pure lines of the exterior are transferred to the design of the furniture.

Für den Entwurf dieses Hauses wurde JUMA gebeten, einen kompakten, alltagstauglichen Grundriss zu entwickeln. Das Ergebnis ist ein eher kubisches Volumen, das durch ein lebhaftes Spiel von kontrastierenden Materialien belebt wird.

Da das Haus von der Straße zurückgesetzt ist, schufen die Architekten eine visuelle Verbindung zwischen dem vorderen und dem hinteren Innenhof. Zu diesem Zweck verläuft eine robuste Betonmauer entlang der Vorderseite des Geländes. Die Wand setzt sich im Inneren des Hauses fort - entlang der Ecke des Schreibtisches und des Wohnzimmers - und endet schließlich im hinteren Bereich, parallel zum Schwimmbad. Entlang dieser Wand akzentuieren große Glasflächen das architektonische Bild und schaffen Transparenz und offene Sichtachsen.

Im Inneren tragen die Oberflächen zu einem nüchternen, minimalistischen Erscheinungsbild bei. Die Zement- und Betonwände kontrastieren mit dem schwarzen Holz, das in der Küche und im Esszimmer dominiert, und dem naturfarbenen Holz in den Schlafzimmern und Waschräumen. Die klaren Linien des Äußeren werden auf das Design der Möbel übertragen.

Pour la conception de cette maison, il a été demandé à JUMA de développer un plan compact adapté à la vie quotidienne. Le résultat est un volume plutôt cubique, animé par un jeu vif de matériaux contrastés.

La maison étant en retrait de la rue, les architectes ont créé un lien visuel entre la cour avant et la cour arrière. À cette fin, un solide mur de béton longe la façade du site. Le mur se poursuit à l'intérieur de la maison - le long du coin du bureau et du salon - pour se terminer finalement à l'arrière, parallèlement à la piscine. Le long de ce mur, de grandes sections de verre accentuent l'image architecturale, créant une transparence et des lignes de vue ouvertes.

À l'intérieur, les finitions contribuent à une apparence sobre et minimaliste. Les murs en ciment et en béton contrastent avec le bois noir qui domine la cuisine et la salle à manger, et le bois de couleur naturelle dans les chambres et les salles de bains. Les lignes pures de l'extérieur se retrouvent dans le design du mobilier.

Para el diseño de esta casa, se pidió a JUMA que desarrolle una planta compacta y apta para la vida diaria. El resultado es un volumen más bien cúbico, animado por un vívido juego de materiales contrastados.

Dado que la casa se encuentra alejada de la calle, los arquitectos crearon una conexión visual entre el patio delantero y el trasero. Para ello se planteó un robusto muro de hormigón que recorre la parte delantera del solar. La pared continúa por el interior de la casa, a lo largo de la esquina del escritorio y la sala de estar, para terminar finalmente en la zona trasera, paralela a la piscina. A lo largo de esta pared, hay grandes secciones de cristal que acentúan la imagen arquitectónica, creando transparencia y líneas de visión abiertas.

En el interior los acabados contribuyen a una apariencia sobria y minimalista. Las paredes de cemento y hormigón contrastan con la madera de color negro que domina en la cocina y el comedor, y de color natural en las habitaciones y lavabos. Las líneas puras de exterior se trasladan al diseño del mobiliario.

Marlene Uldschmidt studied architecture at the Hawk University of Applied Sciences and Arts in Germany. After several years working on conservation projects, she founded her studio in the Algarve in 2005. She is a member of the Architektenkammer Germany, the Association of Architects Portugal, and the Royal Institute of British Architects, RIBA. The architect grew up in a medieval town in Germany, where almost everything was made by local craftsmen and the memory of this work is an important factor in her approach. Her time at the Werkbund Werkstatt allowed her to experiment with various materials and their possible applications. The idea behind the firm's work is that architecture and design should be in context with the habitat, topography and heritage of the site. The firm has received several awards and has recently shown its work in an exhibition entitled "Portfolio."

Marlene Uldschmidt studierte Architektur an der Hawk University of Applied Sciences and Arts in Deutschland. Nachdem sie mehrere Jahre an Konservierungsprojekten gearbeitet hatte, gründete sie 2005 ihr Studio an der Algarve. Sie ist Mitglied der Architektenkammer Deutschland, des portugiesischen Architektenverbandes und des Royal Institute of British Architects (RIBA). Die Architektin wuchs in einer mittelalterlichen Stadt in Deutschland auf, in der fast alles von lokalen Handwerkern hergestellt wurde, und die Erinnerung an diese Arbeit ist ein wichtiger Faktor in ihrem Ansatz. Ihre Zeit in der Werkbund-Werkstatt ermöglichte es ihr, mit verschiedenen Materialien und deren Anwendungsmöglichkeiten zu experimentieren. Die Idee hinter der Arbeit des Büros ist, dass Architektur und Design im Zusammenhang mit dem Lebensraum, der Topographie und dem Erbe des Ortes stehen sollten. Das Büro hat mehrere Auszeichnungen erhalten und seine Arbeiten kürzlich in einer Ausstellung mit dem Titel „Portfolio" gezeigt.

Marlene Uldschmidt a étudié l'architecture à l'université des sciences appliquées et des arts de Hawk, en Allemagne. Après avoir travaillé plusieurs années sur des projets de conservation, elle a fondé son studio en Algarve en 2005. Elle est membre de l'Architektenkammer Allemagne, de l'Association des architectes du Portugal et du Royal Institute of British Architects, RIBA. L'architecte a grandi dans une ville médiévale d'Allemagne, où presque tout était fabriqué par des artisans locaux, et le souvenir de ce travail est un facteur important dans son approche. Son séjour au Werkbund Werkstatt lui a permis d'expérimenter divers matériaux et leurs applications possibles. L'idée qui sous-tend le travail de l'entreprise est que l'architecture et le design doivent être en harmonie avec l'habitat, la topographie et le patrimoine du site. Le cabinet a reçu plusieurs prix et a récemment présenté ses travaux dans une exposition intitulée « Portfolio ».

Marlene Uldschmidt estudió arquitectura en la Universidad Hawk de Ciencias Aplicadas y Arte de Alemania. Tras haberse dedicado varios años a proyectos de conservación, fundó su estudio en Algarve, en 2005. Es miembro de la Architektenkammer Germany, de la Association of Architects Portugal, y del Royal Institute of British Architects, RIBA. La arquitecta creció en una ciudad medieval de Alemania, donde casi todo era fabricado por artesanos locales y el recuerdo de este trabajo es un factor importante en su enfoque. El tiempo que pasó en el Werkbund Werkstatt le permitió experimentar con diversos materiales y sus posibles aplicaciones. La idea que subyace al trabajo de la firma es que la arquitectura y el diseño deben estar en contexto con el hábitat, la topografía y el patrimonio del lugar. La firma ha recibido varios premios y recientemente, ha mostrado su trabajo en una exposición titulada «Portfolio».

MARLENE ULDSCHMIDT ARCHITECTS

MARLENE ULDSCHMIDT

FERRAGUDO, PORTUGAL
WWW.MARLENEULDSCHMIDT.COM

VALE DE MARGEM HOUSE

ALGARVE, PORTUGAL

Photos © Fernando Guerra | FG+SG

This single-storey country house is located in a rural area of the Algarve. The house is an extension to a traditional Portuguese L-shaped farmhouse with small rooms and windows. The new construction, of 120 m², consists of an additional wing with geometric lines and white colour that takes advantage of the open orientation to the west.
The difficult topography of the site was integrated into the concept from an early stage. This has made it possible to generate different levels in the interior of the building that connect the spaces in the open plan.
Large glazed sliding surfaces communicate the purity of the flowing interior with the irregular and rugged surroundings. A long outer retaining wall wraps around the main building like a protective mantle. This wall was built with stone that had been excavated during the construction process.
The floor is covered with locally sourced clay tiles. This material was also chosen to cover the flat roof of the new wing, providing a walkable surface and a lookout onto the surrounding farmland.

Dieses einstöckige Landhaus befindet sich in einer ländlichen Gegend der Algarve. Das Haus ist ein Anbau an ein traditionelles portugiesisches Bauernhaus in L-Form mit kleinen Räumen und Fenstern. Der 120 Quadratmeter große Neubau besteht aus einem zusätzlichen Flügel mit geometrischen Linien und weißer Farbe, der sich die offene Ausrichtung nach Westen zunutze macht.
Die schwierige Topografie des Geländes wurde bereits in einem frühen Stadium in das Konzept integriert. Dadurch konnten im Inneren des Gebäudes verschiedene Ebenen geschaffen werden, die die Räume im offenen Grundriss miteinander verbinden.
Große verglaste Schiebeflächen vermitteln die Reinheit des fließenden Innenraums mit der unregelmäßigen und rauen Umgebung. Eine lange äußere Stützmauer legt sich wie ein Schutzmantel um das Hauptgebäude. Diese Mauer wurde aus Steinen errichtet, die beim Bau ausgegraben wurden.
Der Boden ist mit Tonfliesen aus der Region ausgelegt. Dieses Material wurde auch für die Eindeckung des Flachdachs des neuen Flügels gewählt, das eine begehbare Oberfläche und einen Ausblick auf das umliegende Ackerland bietet.

Cette maison de campagne de plain-pied est située dans une zone rurale de l'Algarve. La maison est une extension d'une ferme traditionnelle portugaise en forme de L avec des petites pièces et des fenêtres. La nouvelle construction, de 120 m², consiste en une aile supplémentaire aux lignes géométriques et de couleur blanche qui tire parti de l'orientation ouverte vers l'ouest.
La topographie difficile du site a été intégrée au concept dès le début. Cela a permis de générer différents niveaux à l'intérieur du bâtiment qui relient les espaces dans le plan ouvert.
De grandes surfaces coulissantes vitrées font communiquer la pureté de l'intérieur fluide avec l'environnement irrégulier et accidenté. Un long mur de soutènement extérieur entoure le bâtiment principal comme un manteau protecteur. Ce mur a été construit avec des pierres qui avaient été excavées pendant le processus de construction.
Le sol est recouvert de carreaux d'argile d'origine locale. Ce matériau a également été choisi pour recouvrir le toit plat de la nouvelle aile, offrant une surface praticable et un point de vue sur les terres agricoles environnantes.

Esta casa de campo de una sola planta está situada en una zona rural del Algarve. La vivienda, es una extensión a una granja tradicional portuguesa en forma de L con habitaciones y ventanas pequeñas. La nueva construcción, de 120 m², consta de un ala adicional de líneas geométricas y de color blanco que aprovecha la orientación abierta al oeste.
La difícil topografía del lugar se integró en el concepto desde una fase temprana. Eso ha permitido generar diferentes niveles en el interior del edificio que van conectando los espacios en la planta abierta.
Grandes superficies deslizantes acristaladas comunican la pureza del interior fluido con el entorno irregular y escabroso. Un largo muro de contención exterior envuelve el edificio principal como un manto protector. Esta pared se construyó con la piedra que se había excavado durante el proceso de construcción.
El suelo está revestido con baldosas de arcilla de origen local. También se eligió este material para cubrir el tejado plano de la nueva ala, proporcionando una superficie transitable y un mirador hacia las tierras de cultivo circundantes.

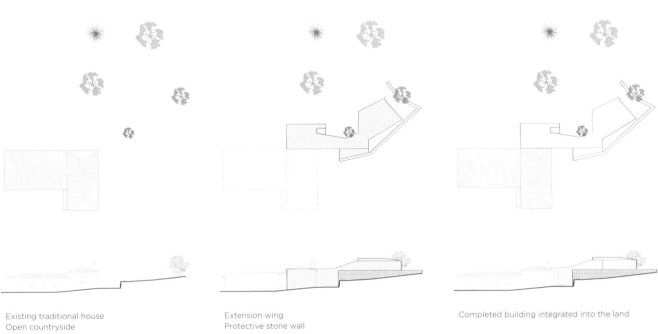

Existing traditional house
Open countryside

Extension wing
Protective stone wall

Completed building integrated into the land

VASCO DA GAMA 26 GALLERY

ALGARVE, PORTUGAL

Photos © Fernando Guerra | FG+SG

The studio had the opportunity to renovate one of the untouched buildings in Vasco da Gama Street, one of the main streets in the village of Ferragudo, located in the Algarve region, southern Portugal. The client's brief was to renovate and convert an adobe building, which was completely dilapidated but retained all its original features, into an exhibition gallery and living space.

The building had the particularity of being connected to the dock through a long and narrow corridor, a space that was used as a boat repair workshop. In fact, the two-storey building had a former boat store on the ground floor and an adult school on the first floor.

In the new functional programme, a gallery was created on the ground floor —which gave the project its name Galeria Vasco da Gama 26— open to the public and benefiting from two entrances. The upper floor was transformed into a loft studio that benefits from a terrace created above the long room.

The spacious and bright interior is an open space under a pinewood roof. The kitchen, bathroom and storage spaces are concealed within a white volume with a sliding door.

Das Studio hatte die Gelegenheit, eines der unberührten Gebäude in der Vasco-da-Gama-Straße zu renovieren, einer der Hauptstraßen des Dorfes Ferragudo in der Algarve-Region im Süden Portugals. Die Aufgabe des Auftraggebers bestand darin, ein Lehmgebäude, das völlig verfallen war, aber noch alle ursprünglichen Merk-male aufwies, zu renovieren und in eine Ausstellungsgalerie und einen Wohnbereich umzuwandeln.

Das Gebäude wies die Besonderheit auf, dass es durch einen langen und schmalen Korridor mit dem Hafen verbunden war, einem Raum, der als Bootsreparaturwerkstatt genutzt wurde. In dem zweistöckigen Gebäude befand sich im Erdgeschoss ein ehemaliges Bootslager und im ersten Stock eine Schule für Erwachsene.

Im Rahmen des neuen Funktionsprogramms wurde im Erdgeschoss eine Galerie eingerichtet, die dem Projekt den Namen Galeria Vasco da Gama 26 gab, die für die Öffentlichkeit zugänglich ist und über zwei Eingänge verfügt. Das Obergeschoss wurde in ein Loft-atelier umgewandelt, das von einer über dem langen Raum an gelegten Terrasse profitiert.

Das geräumige und helle Innere ist ein offener Raum unter einem Dach aus Kiefernholz. Die Küche, das Bad und die Abstellräume sind in einem weißen Volumen mit Schiebetür verborgen.

Le studio a eu l'occasion de rénover l'un des bâtiments intacts de la rue Vasco da Gama, l'une des rues principales du village de Ferragudo, situé dans la région de l'Algarve, au sud du Portugal. Le client avait pour mission de rénover et de convertir un bâtiment en pisé, complètement délabré mais ayant conservé toutes ses caractéristiques d'origine, en une galerie d'exposition et un espace de vie.

Le bâtiment avait la particularité d'être relié au quai par un couloir long et étroit, un espace qui était utilisé comme atelier de réparation de bateaux. En fait, le bâtiment de deux étages comportait un ancien magasin de bateaux au rez-de-chaussée et une école pour adultes au premier étage.

Dans le nouveau programme fonctionnel, une galerie a été créée au rez-de-chaussée - qui a donné au projet son nom de Galeria Vasco da Gama 26 - ouverte au public et bénéficiant de deux entrées. L'étage supérieur a été transformé en un studio loft qui bénéficie d'une terrasse créée au-dessus de la salle longue.

L'intérieur, spacieux et lumineux, est un espace ouvert sous un toit en bois de pin. La cuisine, la salle de bain et les espaces de rangement sont dissimulés dans un volume blanc avec une porte coulissante.

El estudio tuvo la oportunidad de renovar uno de los edificios intactos de la calle Vasco da Gama, una de las calles principales del pueblo de Ferragudo, situado en la región del Algarve, al sur de Portugal. El encargo del cliente era renovar y convertir un edificio de adobe, que estaba completamente deteriorado pero que conservaba todas sus características originales, en una galería de exposiciones y un espacio para vivir.

El edificio tenía la particularidad de estar conectado al muelle a través de un largo y estrecho pasillo, un espacio que se utilizaba como taller de reparación de barcos. De hecho, el edificio de dos plantas tenía un antiguo almacén de barcos en la planta baja y una escuela de adultos en el primer piso.

En el nuevo programa funcional, se creó una galería en la planta baja, que dio al proyecto el nombre de Galería Vasco da Gama 26, abierta al público y con dos entradas. La planta superior se transformó en un estudio tipo loft que se beneficia de una terraza creada sobre la sala de forma alargada.

El interior, amplio y luminoso, es un espacio abierto bajo un techo de madera de pino. La cocina, el cuarto de baño y los espacios de almacenamiento están ocultos dentro de un volumen blanco con una puerta corredera.

Marty Chou received a Bachelor of Architecture degree from the University of Toronto (Canada) in 2002 and a Master of Advanced Architectural Design degree from Columbia University (New York) in 2005. Since 2016, he has been teaching architectural design at the National Taipei University of Technology (NTUT) in Taiwan.

The firm Marty Chou Architecture was founded in 2013, and since then has aimed to follow the path of the art of clarity, and the beauty of simplicity in architecture. His works are featured in international publications and he has won the WIN Awards 2018, A' Design Award and Conpetition 2020, Taiwan Interior Design Award (TID) 2017/2020 /2021, and the 2021 Architizer A+ award.

Marty Chou erwarb 2002 einen Bachelor of Architecture an der Universität von Toronto (Kanada) und 2005 einen Master of Advanced Architectural Design an der Columbia University (New York). Seit 2016 unterrichtet er Architektur-design an der National Taipei University of Technology (NTUT) in Taiwan.

Das Büro Marty Chou Architecture wurde 2013 gegründet und hat sich seither zum Ziel gesetzt, den Weg der Kunst der Klarheit und der Schönheit der Einfachheit in der Architektur zu beschreiten. Seine Arbeiten werden in internationalen Publikationen vorgestellt und er hat den WIN Awards 2018, den A' Design Award and Conpetition 2020, den Taiwan Interior Design Award (TID) 2017/2020 /2021 und den Architizer A+ Award 2021 gewonnen.

Marty Chou a obtenu une licence en architecture de l'université de Toronto (Canada) en 2002 et une maîtrise en concep-tion architecturale avancée de l'université Columbia (New York) en 2005. Depuis 2016, il enseigne la conception archi-tecturale à l'université nationale de technologie de Taipei (NTUT), à Taïwan.

Le cabinet Marty Chou Architecture a été fondé en 2013, et depuis lors, il vise à suivre la voie de l'art de la clarté, et de la beauté de la simplicité en architecture. Ses œuvres sont présentées dans des publications internationales et il a remporté le WIN Awards 2018, le prix et le concours A' Design 2020, le prix du design intérieur de Taïwan (TID) 2017/2020 /2021, et le prix Architizer A+ 2021.

Marty Chou se licenció en Arquitectura en la Universidad de Toronto (Canadá) en 2002 y obtuvo un máster en Diseño Arquitectónico Avanzado en la Universidad de Columbia (Nueva York) en 2005. Desde el año 2016, ha estado enseñan-do diseño arquitectónico en la Universidad Nacional de Tecnología de Taipei (NTUT), en Taiwán.

La firma Marty Chou Architecture fue fundada en 2013, y desde entonces ha tenido como propósito seguir el camino del arte de la claridad, y la belleza de la simplicidad en la arquitectura. Sus obras aparecen en publicaciones internacionales y ha ganado los premios WIN Awards 2018, A' Design Award and Conpetition 2020, Taiwan Interior Design Award (TID) 2017/2020 /2021, y el premio 2021 Architizer A+.

MARTY CHOU ARCHITECTURE

MARTY CHOU

TAIPEI, TAIWAN
WWW.MARTYCHOU.COM

KOA APARTMENT

TAIPEI, TAIWAN

Photos © Kyle Yu Photo Studio

This 90 m², fully open-plan flat reflects the life of an urban family in its current phase. The owners, a young couple with two children, wanted a home that was different from the traditional concept. Their priority was to have space for their children to run around freely and a large table to spend time together. The most important thing was to have a simple, calm and light-filled setting. Based on that premise the architect designed a flat without defined divisions in which it is possible to do almost anything.

Concealed cupboards along the four main walls and a strip of windows reinforce the open-plan, minimalist character of the flat. Through these recessed openings, constant northern light streams in throughout the day. At night when they are closed, they become private bedrooms. The sanitary space and its parts create a geometric play of volumes with a framed composition. A 3,5 m worktop acts as a visual anchor and serves as a multifunctional table. Its abstract appearance and the furniture are reminiscent of a stone slab, a block of wood and clay objects, and are therefore treated as sculptures in space.

Diese 90 m², völlig offen gestaltete Wohnung spiegelt das Leben einer städtischen Familie in ihrer jetzigen Phase wider. Die Bauherren, ein junges Paar mit zwei Kindern, wollten ein Haus, das sich vom traditionellen Konzept unterscheidet. Ihre Priorität war es, Platz für ihre Kinder zu haben, damit sie frei herumlaufen können, und einen großen Tisch, um Zeit miteinander zu verbringen. Das Wichtigste war eine einfache, ruhige und lichtdurchflutete Umgebung. Ausgehend von dieser Prämisse entwarf der Architekt eine Wohnung ohne definierte Unterteilungen, in der man fast alles machen kann.

Verdeckte Schränke entlang der vier Hauptwände und ein Fensterband verstärken den offenen, minimalistischen Charakter der Wohnung. Durch diese eingelassenen Öffnungen strömt den ganzen Tag über konstantes Nordlicht ein. Nachts, wenn sie geschlossen sind, werden sie zu privaten Schlafzimmern. Der Sanitärraum und seine Teile bilden ein geometrisches Spiel von Volumen mit einer gerahmten Komposition. Eine 3,5 m. lange Arbeitsplatte dient als optischer Anker und ist gleichzeitig ein multifunktionaler Tisch. Seine abstrakte Erscheinung und die Möbel erinnern an eine Steinplatte, einen Holzblock und Tonobjekte und werden daher als Skulpturen im Raum behandelt.

Cet appartement de 90 m², entièrement ouvert, reflète la vie d'une famille urbaine dans sa phase actuelle. Les propriétaires, un jeune couple avec deux enfants, souhaitaient une maison différente du concept traditionnel. Leur priorité était d'avoir un espace pour que leurs enfants puissent courir librement et une grande table pour passer du temps ensemble. Le plus important était d'avoir un cadre simple, calme et lumineux. Partant de ce principe, l'architecte a conçu un appartement sans divisions définies, dans lequel il est possible de faire presque tout.

Des placards dissimulés le long des quatre murs principaux et une bande de fenêtres renforcent le caractère ouvert et minimaliste de l'appartement. Grâce à ces ouvertures en retrait, la lumière du nord pénètre en permanence tout au long de la journée. La nuit, lorsqu'elles sont fermées, elles deviennent des chambres privées. L'espace sanitaire et ses parties créent un jeu géométrique de volumes avec une composition encadrée. Un plan de travail de 3,5 m fait office d'ancrage visuel et sert de table multifonctionnelle. Son aspect abstrait et son mobilier rappellent une dalle de pierre, un bloc de bois et des objets en argile, et sont donc traités comme des sculptures dans l'espace.

Este apartamento de 90 m² y planta completamente abierta refleja la vida de una familia urbana en su etapa actual. Los propietarios, una pareja joven con dos niños, deseaban un hogar diferente al concepto tradicional. Su prioridad era tener espacio para que sus hijos corran libremente y una mesa grande en la que pasar tiempo juntos. Lo más importante era contar con un ambiente de configuración simple, tranquilo y lleno de luz. Basándose en esa premisa el arquitecto diseñó un piso sin divisiones definidas en el que es posible hacer casi cualquier cosa.

Los armarios ocultos a lo largo de las cuatro paredes principales y una franja de ventanas refuerzan el carácter diáfano y minimalista de la vivienda. A través de estas aperturas empotradas ingresa luz del norte constante durante todo el día. Por la noche cuando se cierran, se convierten en dormitorios privados. El espacio sanitario y sus piezas crean un juego geométrico de volúmenes con una composición enmarcada. Una encimera de 3,5 m funciona como ancla visual y sirve de mesa multifuncional. Su aspecto abstracto y los muebles recuerdan a una losa de piedra, un bloque de madera y unos objetos de arcilla, y por eso son tratados como esculturas en el espacio.

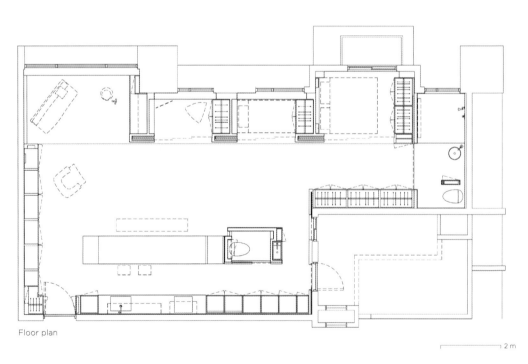

Floor plan

⌐   ⌐ 2 m

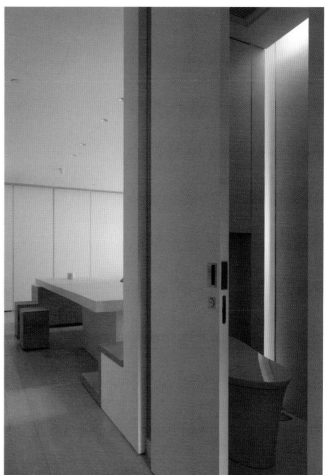

Maya Sheinberger Interior Design oversees a wide range of projects focused on luxury residences and corporate offices. The firm was established in 2012 by interior designer Maya Sheinberger. An honours graduate of the Interior Design Department, College of Management, the designer has completed specialisations at the IUAV University of Venice and La Cambre School of Arts, Brussels.

The studio offers complete project management and planning, from concept creation to execution. Its work prioritises the client's needs and focuses on the creation of efficiently organised spaces. It therefore provides comprehensive design solutions from the plan to the realisation of your vision. Based on the concepts established in an open dialogue with the client, the firm plans a design that takes into account the client's deadlines and financial needs.

Maya Sheinberger Interior Design betreut eine breite Palette von Projekten, die sich auf Luxuswohnungen und Firmenbüros konzentrieren. Das Unternehmen wurde 2012 von der Innenarchitektin Maya Sheinberger gegründet. Die Designerin ist Absolventin des Fachbereichs Innenarchitektur am College of Management und hat sich an der IUAV Universität Venedig und an der La Cambre School of Arts in Brüssel spezialisiert.

Das Studio bietet ein komplettes Projektmanagement und eine komplette Planung, von der Konzeption bis zur Ausführung. Ihre Arbeit stellt die Bedürfnisse des Kunden in den Vordergrund und konzentriert sich auf die Schaffung von effizient organisierten Räumen. Sie bietet daher umfassende Designlösungen von der Planung bis zur Verwirklichung Ihrer Visionen. Auf der Grundlage der in einem offenen Dialog mit dem Kunden erarbeiteten Konzepte plant das Unternehmen einen Entwurf, der die zeitlichen und finanziellen Anforderungen des Kunden berücksichtigt.

Maya Sheinberger Interior Design supervise un large éventail de projets axés sur les résidences de luxe et les bureaux d'entreprise. Le cabinet a été créé en 2012 par l'architecte d'intérieur Maya Sheinberger. Diplômée avec mention du département de design d'intérieur du College of Management, la designer a suivi des spécialisations à l'université IUAV de Venise et à l'école des arts de La Cambre, à Bruxelles.

Le studio propose une gestion et une planification complètes des projets, de la création du concept à l'exécution. Son travail donne la priorité aux besoins du client et se concentre sur la création d'espaces efficacement organisés. Elle fournit donc des solutions de conception complètes, du plan à la réalisation de votre vision. Sur la base des concepts établis dans le cadre d'un dialogue ouvert avec le client, l'entreprise planifie une conception qui tient compte de ses délais et de ses besoins financiers.

Maya Sheinberger Interior Design supervisa una amplia gama de proyectos enfocados a residencias de lujo y oficinas corporativas. La firma fue creada en 2012 por la diseñadora de interiores Maya Sheinberger. Graduada con honores del Departamento de Diseño de Interiores, del College of Management, la diseñadora ha realizado especializaciones en la Universidad IUAV de Venecia y La Cambre School of Arts, en Bruselas.

El estudio ofrece la gestión y planificación completa del proyecto, desde la creación del concepto hasta la ejecución. Su trabajo prioriza las necesidades de los clientes y se centra en la creación de espacios organizados de forma eficiente. Por ello proporciona soluciones de diseño integrales desde el plano, hasta la realización de su visión. A partir de los conceptos establecidos en un diálogo abierto con el cliente, la firma planifica un diseño que tenga en cuenta sus plazos y necesidades financieras.

MAYA SHEINBERGER
INTERIOR DESIGN

MAYA SHEINBERGER

TEL AVIV, ISRAEL
WWW.MAYASHEIN.COM

RB APARTMENT

TEL AVIV, ISRAEL

Photos © Itay Benit

Deciding to leave the city centre for a quieter life, a young family bought this property on the outskirts of Tel Aviv. The flat was very old and had to be adapted to the new dynamic of the couple, who were soon to have their first child and were looking for a cosy, open-plan home. The designer opted for finishes in white, light grey and mint green, with textural variations, furniture with pure lines and a fluid layout that lets in light. The entrance to the home is a space without divisions where the living room, dining room and kitchen are located. The floor is herringbone oak. A large custom-made black iron bookcase dominates the room. The extremely thin shelves give it a light appearance. The bench along the window was covered with MDF boards to create a cement-like finish. At the other end of the room is the minimalist and timeless kitchen with white cabinets and a grey terrazzo-like worktop that is continued on part of the wall. In the master suite, a glass partition with a sliding door was installed to create a division with the bathroom. This allows a slight redistribution of the spaces and a subtle enlargement of the bedroom.

Entschlossen, das Stadtzentrum zu verlassen und ein ruhigeres Leben zu führen, kaufte eine junge Familie diese Immobilie am Rande von Tel Aviv. Die Wohnung war sehr alt und musste an die neue Dynamik des Paares angepasst werden, das kurz vor der Geburt seines ersten Kindes stand und ein gemütliches, offenes Zuhause suchte. Die Designerin entschied sich für Oberflächen in Weiß, Hellgrau und Mintgrün mit unterschiedlichen Texturen, für Möbel mit klaren Linien und für eine fließende, lichtdurchlässige Gestaltung. Der Eingang des Hauses ist ein Raum ohne Unterteilung, in dem sich das Wohnzimmer, das Esszimmer und die Küche befinden. Der Boden ist aus Eichenholz im Fischgrätmuster. Ein großes maßgefertigtes schwarzes Eisenregal dominiert den Raum. Die extrem dünnen Regalböden verleihen ihm ein leichtes Aussehen. Die Bank entlang des Fensters wurde mit MDF-Platten verkleidet, um eine zementähnliche Oberfläche zu schaffen. Am anderen Ende des Raumes befindet sich die minimalistische, zeitlose Küche mit weißen Schränken und einer grauen Arbeitsplatte im Terrazzo-Stil, die sich auf einem Teil der Wand fortsetzt. In der Master-Suite wurde eine Glastrennwand mit einer Schiebetür eingebaut, um eine Trennung zum Badezimmer zu schaffen. Dies ermöglicht eine leichte Umverteilung der Räume und eine subtile Vergrößerung des Schlafzimmers.

Déterminée à quitter le centre ville pour une vie plus tranquille, une jeune famille a acheté cette propriété à la périphérie de Tel Aviv. L'appartement était très ancien et devait être adapté à la nouvelle dynamique du couple, qui allait bientôt avoir son premier enfant et recherchait une maison confortable et ouverte. Le designer a opté pour des finitions en blanc, gris clair et vert menthe, avec des variations de textures, des meubles aux lignes pures et un agencement fluide qui laisse passer la lumière. L'entrée de la maison est un espace sans divisions où se trouvent le salon, la salle à manger et la cuisine. Le sol est en chêne à chevrons. Une grande bibliothèque en fer noir faite sur mesure domine la pièce. Les étagères extrêmement fines lui donnent un aspect léger. Le banc le long de la fenêtre a été recouvert de panneaux MDF pour créer une finition semblable à du ciment. À l'autre bout de la pièce se trouve la cuisine minimaliste et intemporelle avec des armoires blanches et un plan de travail gris de style terrazzo qui se poursuit sur une partie du mur. Dans la suite principale, une cloison en verre avec une porte coulissante a été installée pour créer une séparation avec la salle de bains. Cela permet une légère redistribution des espaces et un élargissement subtil de la chambre.

Decididos a dejar el centro de la ciudad por una vida más tranquila, una joven familia adquirió esta propiedad en las afueras de Tel Aviv. El apartamento era muy antiguo y debía adaptarse a la nueva dinámica de la pareja que pronto tendría a su primer hijo y buscaba un hogar acogedor, diáfano y abierto. La diseñadora se decantó por unos acabados en blanco, gris claro y verde menta, con variantes de texturas, un mobiliario de líneas puras y una distribución fluida que deja pasar la luz. El acceso a la vivienda es un espacio sin divisiones donde está el salón, el comedor y la cocina. El suelo es de madera de roble en espiga. Una gran estantería de hierro negro hecha a medida domina el ambiente. Los estantes extremadamente finos le otorgan una apariencia liviana. El banco a lo largo de la ventana se cubrió con tableros de MDF para crear un acabado similar al cemento. En el otro extremo de la habitación, aparece la cocina minimalista y atemporal con armarios blancos y una encimera gris tipo terrazo que se continúa en parte de la pared. En la suite principal se instaló una mampara de cristal con una puerta corredera para crear una división con el baño. Esto permite una ligera redistribución de los espacios y una sutil ampliación del dormitorio.

Floor plan

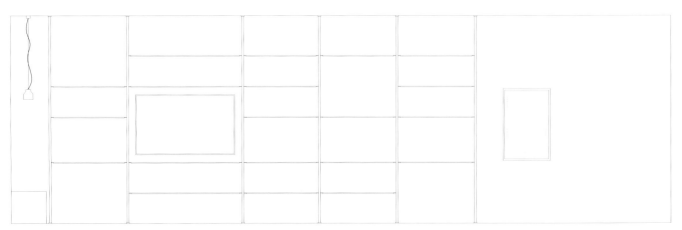

Bookshelf elevation

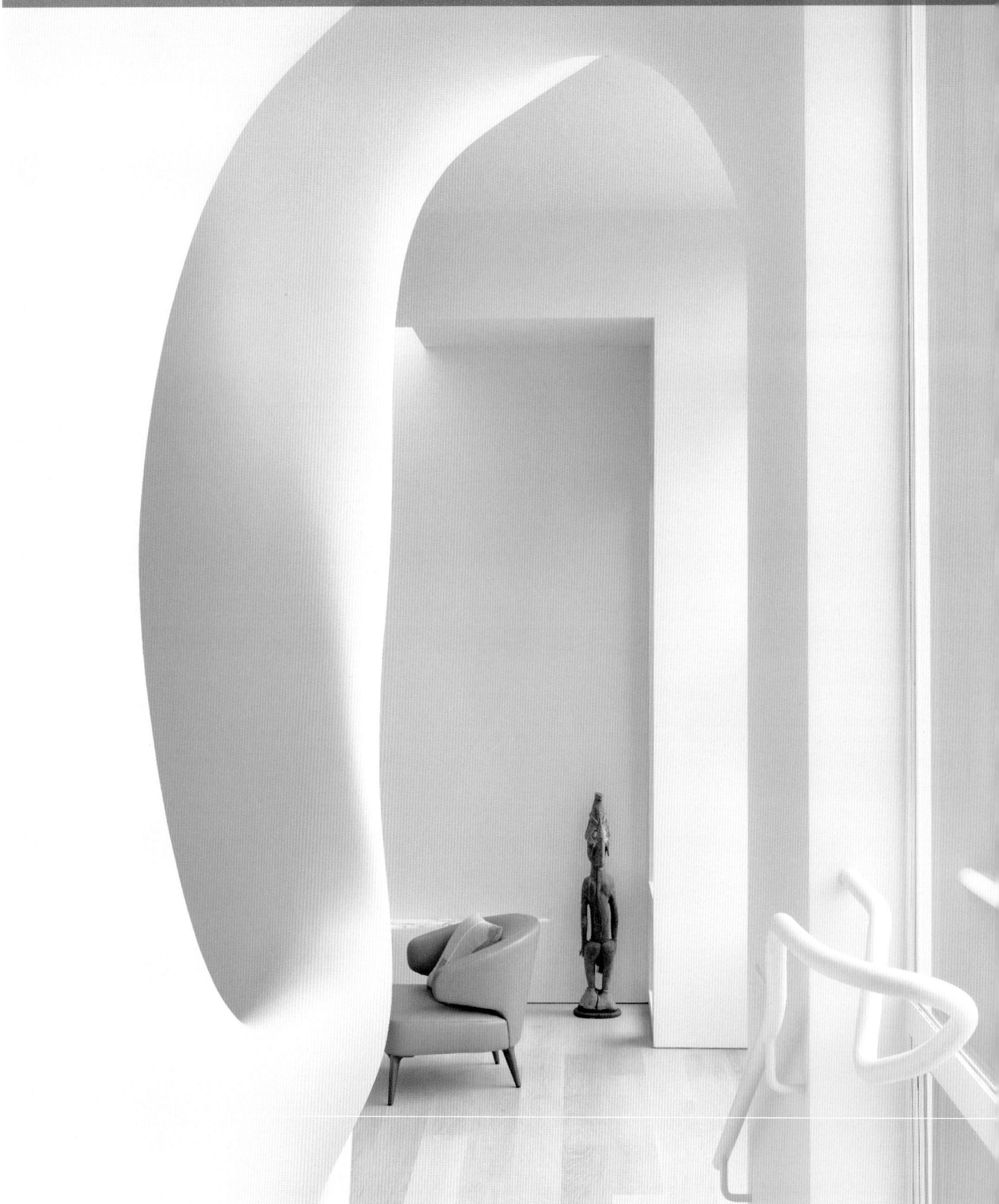

Ogrydziak Prillinger Architects is an architecture and design practice founded by Luke Ogrydziak and Zoë Prillinger in 2004. Both partners hold Masters of Architecture degrees from Princeton University and have taught design at the University of California, Berkley and Harvard University.

The studio believes that architecture influences how people see and live in the world, their perceptions and emotions act as a physical framework for thought. They claim that their strength lies in identifying and creating spatial experiences that make this possible.

OPA has a long list of awards and distinctions, including several from the American Institute of Architects (AIA) San Francisco, AIA California, and the 2018 American Architecture Award from the Atheneum of Chicago.

Ogrydziak Prillinger Architects ist ein Architektur- und Designbüro, das 2004 von Luke Ogrydziak und Zoë Prillinger gegründet wurde. Beide Partner haben einen Master of Architecture der Princeton University und lehrten Design an der University of California, Berkley und der Harvard University.

Das Studio ist der Ansicht, dass Architektur die Art und Weise beeinflusst, wie Menschen die Welt sehen und in ihr leben, ihre Wahrnehmungen und Emotionen, und dass sie als physischer Rahmen für das Denken dient. Daher liege ihre Stärke darin, räumliche Erfahrungen zu identifizieren und zu schaffen, die dies ermöglichen.

OPA hat eine lange Liste von Preisen und Auszeichnungen, darunter mehrere vom American Institute of Architects (AIA) San Francisco, AIA California und den 2018 American Architecture Award des Atheneum of Chicago.

Ogrydziak Prillinger Architects est un cabinet d'architecture et de design fondé par Luke Ogrydziak et Zoë Prillinger en 2004. Les deux partenaires sont titulaires d'une maîtrise en architecture de l'université de Princeton et ont enseigné le design à l'université de Californie, Berkley et à l'université de Harvard.

Le studio estime que l'architecture influence la façon dont les gens voient et vivent dans le monde, leurs perceptions et leurs émotions, et qu'elle agit comme un cadre physique pour la pensée. Ils affirment donc que leur force réside dans l'identification et la création d'expériences spatiales qui rendent cela possible.

L'OPA possède une longue liste de prix et de distinctions, dont plusieurs décernés par l'American Institute of Architects (AIA) San Francisco, l'AIA California et le prix d'architecture américain 2018 de l'Atheneum de Chicago.

Ogrydziak Prillinger Architects es un estudio de arquitectura y diseño fundado por Luke Ogrydziak y Zoë Prillinger en el año 2004. Ambos socios cuentan con un Máster en Arquitectura de la Universidad de Princeton y han impartido estudios de diseño en la Universidad de California, en Berkley y la Universidad de Harvard.

El estudio cree que la arquitectura influye en cómo se ve el mundo y se vive en él, en las percepciones y emociones de las personas, y que actúa como marco físico para el pensamiento. Por tanto, afirman que su punto fuerte es identificar y crear experiencias espaciales que lo hagan posible.

OPA cuenta con una larga lista de premios y distinciones, entre ellos varios otorgados por el American Institute of Architects (AIA) San Francisco, AIA California, y el premio American Architecture 2018 del Atheneum de Chicago.

OPA

LUKE OGRYDZIAK, ZOË PRILLINGER

SAN FRANCISCO, UNITED STATES
WWW.OPARCH.NET

SOFTIE

CALIFORNIA, UNITED STATES

Photos © Naaro & Joe Fletcher

"Why can't architecture be more like nature: changeable, varied and uninhibited", OPA architects asked them-selves when faced with this commission. The project involved the renovation of a modernist house on the edge of a cliff in Mill Valley, north of San Francisco.

A house that would give him the client a sense of freedom, an escape from the conformity of the outside world. So the architects built him a house in the clouds.

White volumes of undulating shapes are freely dispersed throughout the house, dissolving it in different ways. The clouds erode and blur the order of the rational modernist grid, creating a sense of floating and drifting space. Curved walls, moving surfaces, organic arches and vaults replace sharp angles and straight lines.

Moments of softness are found randomly. In fact, the interventions are like a fog that has settled in an irregular way and that, when entering the house, blurs the entrance, runs through the three floors and, like a solitary cloud, is trapped on a protected terrace in the form of an installation.

Warum kann die Architektur nicht mehr wie die Natur sein: wandelbar, vielfältig und ungehemmt, fragten sich die Architekten von OPA, als sie mit diesem Auftrag konfrontiert wurden. Das Projekt umfasste die Renovie-rung eines modernistischen Hauses am Rande einer Klippe in Mill Valley, nördlich von San Francisco.

Der Bauherr wollte ein Haus, das ihm ein Gefühl von Freiheit gibt, eine Flucht vor der Konformität der Außen-welt. Also bauten die Architekten ihm ein Haus in den Wolken.

Weiße Volumen mit wellenförmigen Formen sind frei im Haus verteilt und lösen es auf unterschiedliche Weise auf. Die Wolken erodieren und verwischen die Ordnung des rationalen modernistischen Rasters und schaffen ein Gefühl von schwebendem und treibendem Raum. Gebogene Wände, bewegte Flächen, organische Bögen und Gewölbe ersetzen scharfe Winkel und gerade Linien.

Momente der Weichheit werden zufällig gefunden. In der Tat sind die Interventionen wie ein Nebel, der sich auf unregelmäßige Weise niedergelassen hat und der beim Betreten des Hauses den Eingang verwischt, sich durch die drei Stockwerke zieht und wie eine einsame Wolke auf einer geschützten Terrasse in Form einer Installation gefangen ist.

Pourquoi l'architecture ne peut-elle pas ressembler davantage à la nature : changeante, variée et sans en-traves, se sont demandé les architectes de l'OPA face à cette commande. Le projet consistait à rénover une maison moderniste située au bord d'une falaise à Mill Valley, au nord de San Francisco.

Le client voulait une maison qui lui donnerait un sentiment de liberté, une échappatoire à la conformité du monde extérieur. Les architectes lui ont donc construit une maison dans les nuages.

Des volumes blancs aux formes ondulantes sont librement dispersés dans la maison, la dissolvant de diffé-rentes manières. Les nuages érodent et brouillent l'ordre de la grille moderniste rationnelle, créant un senti-ment d'espace flottant et à la dérive. Les murs courbes, les surfaces mobiles, les arcs et les voûtes organiques remplacent les angles aigus et les lignes droites.

Les moments de douceur sont trouvés au hasard. En fait, les interventions sont comme un brouillard qui s'est installé de manière irrégulière et qui, en entrant dans la maison, brouille l'entrée, traverse les trois étages et, comme un nuage solitaire, est piégé sur une terrasse protégée sous forme d'installation.

¿Por qué la arquitectura no puede ser más parecida a la naturaleza: cambiante, variada y desinhibida?, se preguntaron los arquitectos de OPA cuando se enfrentaron a este encargo. El proyecto implicaba la reforma de una casa modernista emplazada al borde de un acantilado en Mill Valley, al norte de San Francisco.

El cliente quería una casa que le transfiera una sensación de libertad, un escape de la conformidad imperante en el mundo exterior. Así que los arquitectos le construyeron una casa en las nubes.

Volúmenes blancos de formas onduladas se dispersan libremente por toda la casa, y la disuelven de diferen-tes maneras. Las nubes erosionan y desdibujan el orden de la cuadrícula racional modernista, creando una sensación de espacio que flota y está a la deriva. Paredes curvas, superficies en movimiento, arcos orgánicos y bóvedas sustituyen los ángulos pronunciados y las líneas rectas.

Los momentos de suavidad se encuentran aleatoriamente. De hecho, las intervenciones son como una niebla que se ha asentado de forma irregular y que al entrar a la casa desdibuja la entrada, recorre las tres plantas y como una nube solitaria queda atrapada sobre una terraza protegida bajo la forma de una instalación.

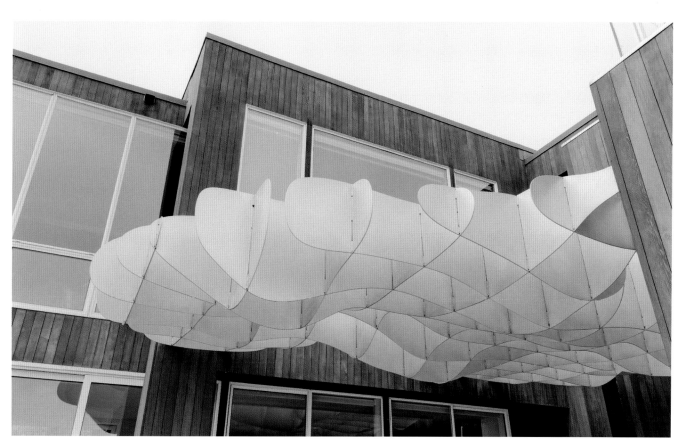

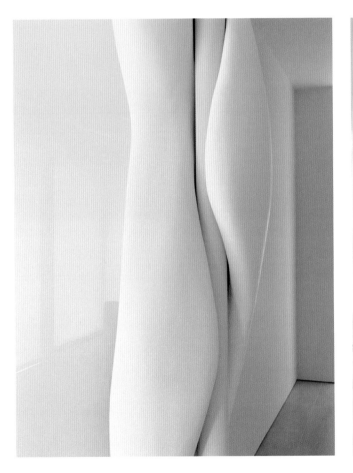

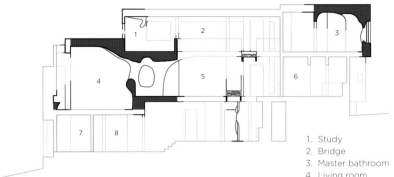

1. Study
2. Bridge
3. Master bathroom
4. Living room
5. Entry
6. Kitchen
7. Bathroom
8. Bedroom

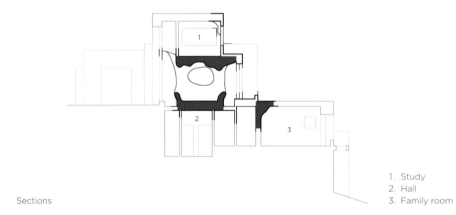

Sections

1. Study
2. Hall
3. Family room

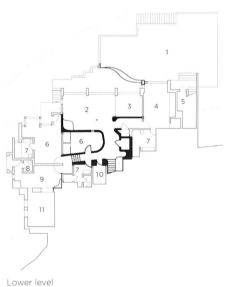

Lower level

1. Pool
2. Family room
3. Exercise
4. Study
5. Stair
6. Bedroom
7. Bathroom
8. WC
9. Den
10. Mechanical
11. Office

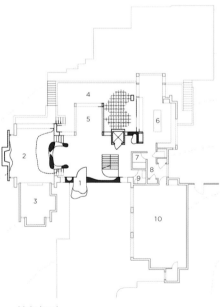

Main level

1. Entry
2. Living room
3. Media room
4. Terrace
5. Dining
6. Kitchen
7. Utility
8. Mud room
9. WC
10. Garage

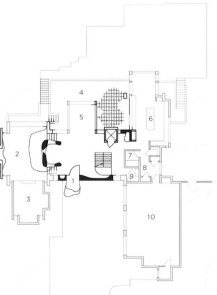

Upper level

1. Study
2. Master bedroom
3. Bridge
4. Closet
5. Master bathroom
6. Terrace

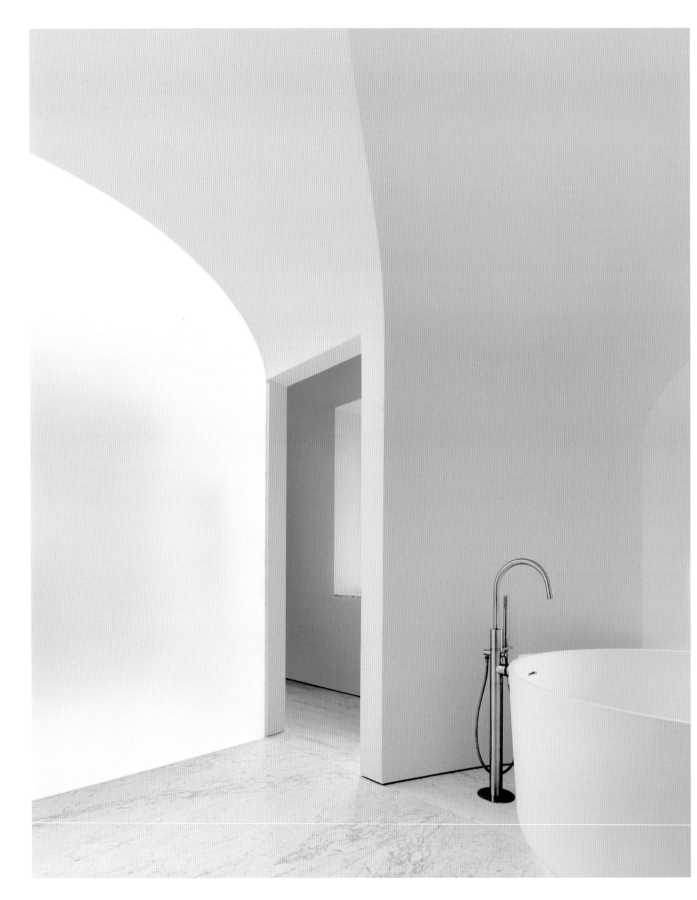

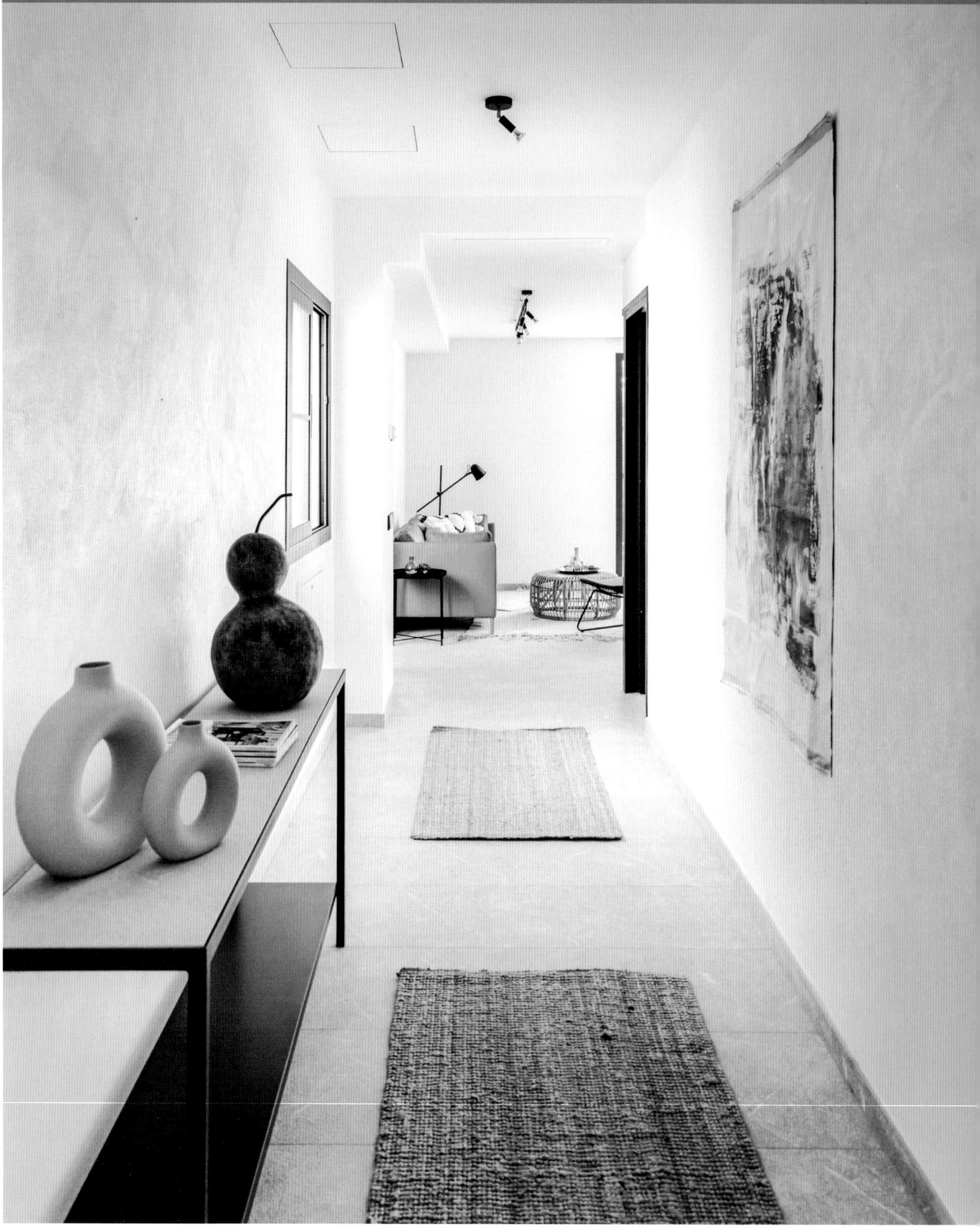

Based in Palma de Mallorca, PMA Studio specialises in the development of architectural projects since 2016. Its founder, architect Pablo Madrid worked for several foreign studios developing international projects. Back in Mallorca, he has focussed in local construction, obtaining a Master's Degree in Urban Planning Law from the University of the Balearic Islands and a Rehabilitation Course from the Balearic Islands Architects Association.

Since its beginnings, PMA STUDIO has been growing steadily, reaching to shape of a young and multidisciplinary team, which aims to innovate in each of its projects.

The company has developed a wide range of projects, both residential and commercial, all of them under a design based on the use of Mediterranean materials and techniques, introducing the advantages of new technologies as well as details with Scandinavian and Asian style influences.

PMA Studio hat seinen Sitz in Palma de Mallorca und ist seit 2016 auf die Entwicklung von Architekturprojekten spezialisiert. Ihr Gründer, der Architekt Pablo Madrid, arbeitete für mehrere ausländische Studios an internationalen Projekten. Zurück auf Mallorca spezialisierte er sich auf das lokale Bauwesen und erwarb einen Master-Abschluss in Stadtplanungsrecht an der Universität der Balearen sowie einen Sanierungskurs der Architektenkammer der Balearen.

Seit seinen Anfängen ist PMA STUDIO stetig gewachsen und hat ein junges und multidisziplinäres Team gebildet, das bei jedem seiner Projekte auf Innovation setzt.

Es handelt sich um Projekte aller Art, sowohl für Wohn- als auch für Geschäftszwecke, die alle auf der Verwendung mediterraner Materialien und Techniken basieren und die Vorteile neuer Technologien sowie Details mit skandinavischen und asiatischen Stileinflüssen beinhalten.

Basé à Palma de Majorque, PMA Studio est spécialisé dans le développement de projets architecturaux depuis 2016. Son fondateur, l'architecte Pablo Madrid, a travaillé pour plusieurs studios étrangers en développant des projets internationaux. De retour à Majorque, il s'est spécialisé dans la construction locale, obtenant une maîtrise en droit de l'urbanisme de l'université des Baléares et un cours de réhabilitation de l'association des architectes des Baléares.

Depuis ses débuts, PMA STUDIO n'a cessé de croître, parvenant à la formation d'une équipe jeune et multidisciplinaire, qui vise à innover dans chacun de ses projets.

La société a développé une large gamme de projets, tant résidentiels que commerciaux, tous sous un design basé sur l'utilisation de matériaux et de techniques méditerranéens, introduisant les avantages des nouvelles technologies ainsi que des détails aux influences de style scandinave et asiatique.

Con sede en Palma de Mallorca, PMA Studio está especializado en el desarrollo de proyectos de arquitectura desde el año 2016. Su fundador, el arquitecto Pablo Madrid trabajó para varios estudios extranjeros desarrollando proyectos internacionales. De regreso a Mallorca, se ha especializado en la construcción local, con la obtención de un Master en Derecho Urbanístico por la Universidad de las Islas Baleares y Curso de Rehabilitación por el Colegio de Arquitectos de las Islas Baleares.

Desde sus inicios, PMA STUDIO ha ido creciendo constantemente, alcanzando la formación de un equipo joven y multidisciplinar, el cual tiene como objetivo la innovación en cada uno de sus proyectos.

Destacan obras de todo tipo, tanto residencial como dotacionales, todos ellos bajo un diseño basado en el uso de materiales y técnicas mediterráneas, introduciendo las ventajas de las nuevas tecnologías así como detalles con influencias de estilo escandinavo y asiático.

PMA STUDIO

PABLO MADRID

PALMA DE MALLORCA, SPAIN
WWW.PMASTUDIO.COM

PORTIXOL I

PALMA DE MALLORCA, SPAIN

Photos © Pernilla Danielsson

This house in the fishing district of Portixol on the island of Mallorca, is the product of a complete renovation of a traditional house between party walls. Despite the very narrow shape of the plot and the fact that it has only two façades, the project manages to create open-plan spaces full of natural light. The living room is located at the back of the plot, right next to the main courtyard. A large glass door extends this space and blurs the boundary between inside and outside. The façade facing the street also has a glass door. The master bedroom is close to the entrance. The second bedroom occupies the narrowest area of the lot, but a glass partition in one corner and a skylight in the ceiling let in light and give it a sense of spaciousness. To achieve a timeless aesthetic, natural materials and tones were used. Ceramic tiles, limestone floors and exposed wooden beams resonate with Mallorcan tradition, while black window frames and accessories connect with the clients' Scandinavian roots. Minimalist Nordic furniture combines with the local straw décor and natural fabrics to create a simple and balanced ambience.

Dieses Haus im Fischerviertel von Portixol auf der Insel Mallorca ist das Ergebnis einer kompletten Renovie-rung eines traditionellen Hauses zwischen zwei Mauern. Trotz der sehr schmalen Form des Grundstücks und der Tatsache, dass es nur zwei Fassaden hat, gelingt es dem Projekt, offene Räume mit viel natürlichem Licht zu schaffen. Das Wohnzimmer befindet sich im hinteren Teil des Grundstücks, direkt neben dem Haupthof. Eine große Glastür erweitert diesen Raum und lässt die Grenze zwischen Innen und Außen verschwimmen. Die der Straße zugewandte Fassade hat ebenfalls eine Glastür. Das Hauptschlafzimmer befindet sich in der Nähe des Eingangs. Das zweite Schlafzimmer nimmt den schmalsten Bereich des Grundstücks ein, aber eine Glastrennwand in einer Ecke und ein Oberlicht an der Decke lassen Licht herein und geben ihm ein Gefühl von Geräumigkeit. Um eine zeitlose Ästhetik zu erreichen, wurden natürliche Materialien und Farbtöne verwendet. Keramikfliesen, Kalksteinböden und freiliegende Holzbalken erinnern an die mallorquinische Tradition, wäh-rend schwarze Fensterrahmen und Accessoires die skandinavischen Wurzeln der Bauherren widerspiegeln. Minimalistische nordische Möbel verbinden sich mit dem lokalen Strohdekor und natürlichen Stoffen zu einem schlichten und ausgewogenen Ambiente.

Cette maison située dans le quartier de pêcheurs de Portixol sur l'île de Majorque est le produit d'une rénova-tion complète d'une maison traditionnelle entre murs mitoyens. Malgré la forme très étroite de la parcelle et le fait qu'elle ne possède que deux façades, le projet parvient à créer des espaces ouverts et pleins de lumière naturelle. Le salon est situé à l'arrière du terrain, juste à côté de la cour principale. Une grande porte vitrée pro-longe cet espace et estompe la frontière entre intérieur et extérieur. La façade donnant sur la rue comporte également une porte vitrée. La chambre principale est proche de l'entrée. La deuxième chambre occupe la zone la plus étroite du terrain, mais une cloison en verre dans un coin et un puits de lumière au plafond laissent entrer la lumière et lui donnent une impression d'espace. Pour obtenir une esthétique intemporelle, des ma-tériaux et des tons naturels ont été utilisés. Les carreaux de céramique, les sols en calcaire et les poutres en bois apparentes font écho à la tradition majorquine, tandis que les cadres de fenêtres et les accessoires noirs rappellent les racines scandinaves des clients. Le mobilier nordique minimaliste s'associe au décor local en paille et aux tissus naturels pour créer une ambiance simple et équilibrée.

Esta casa del barrio pesquero de Portixol en la isla de Mallorca, es producto de la renovación completa de una vivienda tradicional entre medianeras. A pesar de la forma muy estrecha del solar y de contar con sólo dos fachadas, el proyecto logra crear espacios diáfanos y llenos de luz natural. Al fondo de la parcela se situó la sala de estar, justo al lado del patio principal. Una amplia puerta de cristal permite extender este espacio y desdibujar el límite entre el interior y el exterior. La fachada que mira hacia la calle también tiene una puerta cristalera. El dormitorio principal está cerca de la entrada. La segunda habitación ocupa el área más estrecha del solar, pero un tabique de cristal en una de las esquinas y una claraboya en el techo dejan pasar la luz y le aportan sensación de amplitud. Para lograr una estética atemporal, se utilizó materiales y tonos naturales. Las baldosas cerámicas, los suelos de piedra caliza y las vigas de madera vista resuenan con la tradición mallor-quina, mientras que los marcos de las ventanas y los accesorios negros conectan con las raíces escandinavas de los clientes. Los muebles nórdicos minimalistas combinan con la decoración local de paja y las telas natu-rales generando un ambiente sencillo y equilibrado.

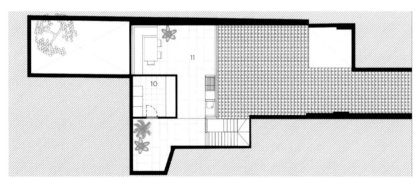

First floor plan

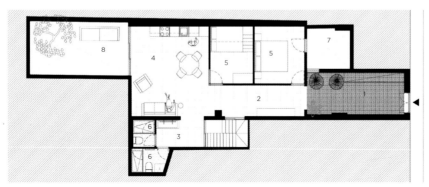

Ground floor plan

1. Entrance
2. Corridor
3. Foyer
4. Living room / kitchen
5. Bedroom
6. Bathroom
7. Inner patio
8. Private patio
9. Stairs
10. Laundry
11. Terrace

Raulino Silva is an architect graduated from the Escola Superior Artística do Porto. Since 2011, he has his own office in Vila do Conde. His work has received several international awards, including the 2A Continental Architectural Awards, organised by 2A Magazine, the International Architecture Awards, promoted by The Chicago Athenaeum Museum of Architecture and Design, the IF Design Awards, arranged by the IF International Forum Design GMBH, the Iconic Awards, coordinated by the German Design Council and the Baku International Architecture Award, promoted by the Order of Architects with the support of the International Union of Architects.
In 2019 he received the medal of merit of the city of Vila do Conde and, in the same year, he was named one of the best young European architects by winning the Europe 40 Under 40 Awards of The European Centre for Architecture Art Design and Urban Studies.

Raulino Silva ist Architekt und studierte an der Escola Superior Artística do Porto. Seit 2011 hat er sein eigenes Büro in Vila do Conde. Seine Arbeiten wurden mit mehreren internationalen Preisen ausgezeichnet, darunter die 2A Continental Architectural Awards, organisiert vom 2A Magazine, die International Architecture Awards, gefördert vom Chicago Athenaeum Museum of Architecture and Design, die IF Design Awards, organisiert von der IF International Forum Design GMBH, die Iconic Awards, organisiert vom Rat für Formgebung und der Baku International Architecture Award, gefördert vom Order of Architects mit Unterstützung der International Union of Architects.
Im Jahr 2019 erhielt er die Verdienstmedaille der Stadt Vila do Conde und wurde im selben Jahr als einer der besten jungen europäischen Architekten mit dem Europe 40 Under 40 Award des European Centre for Architecture Art Design and Urban Studies ausgezeichnet.

Raulino Silva est un architecte diplômé de l'Escola Superior Artística do Porto. Depuis 2011, il dispose de son propre bureau à Vila do Conde. Son travail a reçu plusieurs prix internationaux, notamment les 2A Continental Architectural Awards, organisés par le magazine 2A, les International Architecture Awards, promus par le Chicago Athenaeum Museum of Architecture and Design, les IF Design Awards, organisés par l'IF International Forum Design GMBH, les Iconic Awards, organisés par le German Design Council et le Baku International Architecture Award, promu par l'Ordre des architectes avec le soutien de l'Union internationale des architectes.
En 2019, il a reçu la médaille du mérite de la ville de Vila do Conde et, la même année, il a été désigné comme l'un des meilleurs jeunes architectes européens en remportant les prix Europe 40 Under 40 de The European Centre for Architecture Art Design and Urban Studies.

Raulino Silva es arquitecto por la Escola Superior Artística do Porto. Desde 2011, tiene su propia oficina en Vila do Conde. Su trabajo ha recibido varios premios internacionales, entre los que destacan los 2A Continental Architectural Awards, organizados por la revista 2A Magazine, los International Architecture Awards, promovidos por The Chicago Athenaeum Museum of Architecture and Design, los IF Design Awards, organizados por el IF International Forum Design GMBH, los Iconic Awards, organizados por el German Design Council y el Baku International Architecture Award, promovido por la Orden de Arquitectos con el apoyo de la Unión Internacional de Arquitectos.
En 2019 recibió la medalla al mérito de la ciudad de Vila do Conde y, en el mismo año se le nombró como uno de los mejores arquitectos jóvenes europeos al ganar el Europe 40 Under 40 Awards de The European Centre for Architecture Art Design and Urban Studies.

RAULINO SILVA ARCHITECT

RAULINO SILVA

VILA DO CONDE, PORTUGAL
RAULINOSILVA.BLOGSPOT.COM

ALDOAR HOUSE

PORTO, PORTUGAL

Photos © João Morgado

The Aldoar House is a family residence in the Monte da Ervilha area, near the mouth of the Douro River in Porto. The two-storey house, with a basement, sits on a large and narrow plot of land.

A small garden leads to the main façade and the pedestrian entrance to the house. On the north-facing side, a ramp gives access to the basement and the back of the swimming pool with outdoor seating area. The underground area houses the garage, a laundry room and a guest room opening onto a courtyard. The public areas of the house are concentrated on the first floor: a kitchen and living room opened onto the swimming pool. The upper floor has three suites: two smaller rooms to the east and the master suite with dressing room to the west. On the back floor, there is another bedroom and an office opening onto a large terrace.

Both inside and outside the house, the volumetry of simple lines and great visual impact stand out. Absolute white is used in the interior spaces with high gloss lacquered carpentry. The bathrooms, patios and wood-burning fireplace are finished in white marble. The solid pine floorboards and the staircase slats add a touch of warmth.

Das Haus Aldoar ist eine Familienresidenz in der Gegend von Monte da Ervilha, nahe der Mündung des Douro in Porto. Das zweistöckige, unterkellerte Haus befindet sich auf einem großen, schmalen Grundstück.

Ein kleiner Garten führt zur Hauptfassade und zum Fußgängereingang des Hauses. Auf der Nordseite gelangt man über eine Rampe in den Keller und auf die Rückseite des Swimmingpools mit Außensitzplatz. Im Untergeschoss befinden sich die Garage, eine Waschküche und ein Gästezimmer mit Zugang zu einem Innenhof. Die öffentlichen Bereiche des Hauses befinden sich im ersten Stock: die Küche und das Wohnzimmer mit Blick auf das Schwimmbad.

Im Obergeschoss befinden sich drei Suiten: zwei kleinere Suiten im Osten und die Master-Suite mit Ankleidezimmer im Westen. Im hinteren Stockwerk befinden sich ein weiteres Schlafzimmer und ein Büro mit Zugang zu einer großen Terrasse.

Sowohl im Innen- als auch im Außenbereich des Hauses fallen die Volumetrie der einfachen Linien und die große optische Wirkung auf. In den Innenräumen mit hochglanzlackierten Tischlerarbeiten wird absolutes Weiß verwendet. Die Bäder, die Terrassen und der Kamin sind mit weißem Marmor ausgestattet. Die massiven Kiefernholzdielen und die Latten im Treppenhaus sorgen für einen Hauch von Wärme.

La maison Aldoar est une résidence familiale située dans la région de Monte da Ervilha, près de l'embouchure du fleuve Douro à Porto. La maison a deux étages et un sous-sol et se trouve sur un grand et étroit terrain.

Un petit jardin mène à la façade principale et à l'entrée piétonne de la maison. Sur le côté nord, une rampe donne accès au sous-sol et à l'arrière de la piscine avec un coin salon extérieur. La partie souterraine abrite le garage, une buanderie et une chambre d'amis donnant sur une cour. Les espaces publics de la maison sont concentrés au premier étage : la cuisine et le salon qui s'ouvre sur la piscine.

L'étage supérieur comprend trois suites : deux suites plus petites à l'est et la suite principale avec dressing à l'ouest. À l'étage arrière, il y a une autre chambre et un bureau donnant sur une grande terrasse.

À l'intérieur comme à l'extérieur de la maison, on remarque la volumétrie des lignes simples et le grand impact visuel. Le blanc absolu est utilisé dans les espaces intérieurs avec des menuiseries laquées haute brillance. Les salles de bains, les patios et la cheminée à bois sont en marbre blanc. Les parquets en pin massif des étages et les escaliers à lattes apportent une touche de chaleur.

La Casa Aldoar es una residencia familiar en la zona del Monte da Ervilha, cerca de la desembocadura del río Duero, en Oporto. La vivienda de dos plantas y un sótano, se asienta en una parcela, amplia y estrecha.

A través de un pequeño jardín se accede a la fachada principal y la entrada peatonal a la casa. En el lado orientado al norte, una rampa da acceso al sótano y a la parte posterior de la piscina con sala de estar al aire libre. La zona subterránea alberga el garaje, un lavadero y una habitación para las visitas que se abre a un patio. En la primera planta se concentran las zonas públicas de la casa: la cocina y el salón que da a la piscina. La planta superior tiene tres suites: dos más pequeñas al Este y la principal con vestidor al Oeste. En la planta trasera, hay otro dormitorio y un despacho abierto a una gran terraza.

Tanto en el interior como en el exterior de la casa destaca una volumetría de líneas simples y gran impacto visual. El blanco absoluto se impone en los espacios interiores con carpintería lacada en alto brillo. En los baños, los patios y la chimenea de leña los acabados son de mármol blanco. La tarima de pino macizo en los suelos y las escaleras de lamas, aporta el punto de calidez.

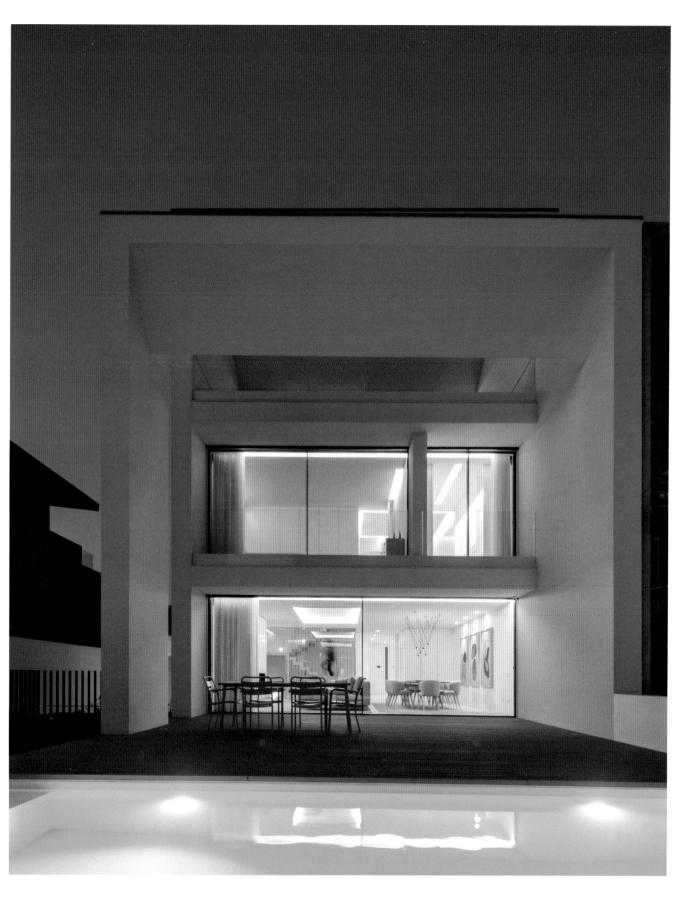

Rooftop plan

Second floor plan

First floor plan

Ground floor plan

Basement plan

1. Garage
2. Storage room
3. Laundry
4. Patio
5. Bedroom
6. Bathroom
7. Technical area
8. Elevator
9. Entry
10. Kitchen
11. Living room
12. Closet
13. Office
14. Pool

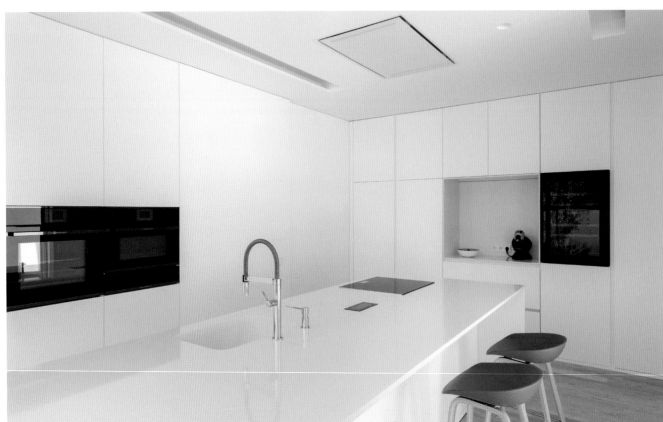

Longitudinal section

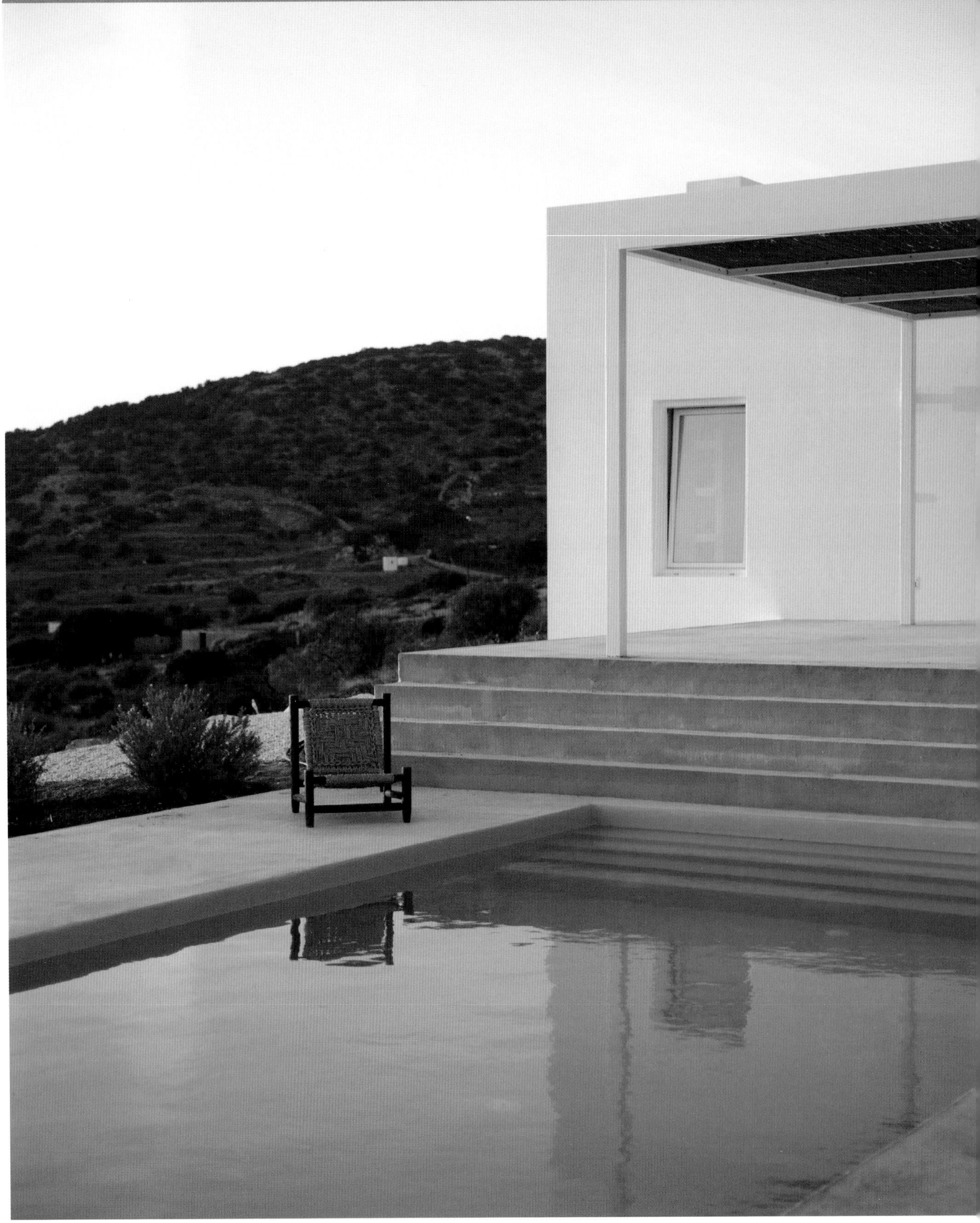

The firm founded by Natasha Deliyianni and Yiorgos Spiridonos in 2007, conceives architecture as a totality in collaboration with all the specialities that complement constructive and artistic creation. The office studies small and large scale projects, both public and private.

Both partners completed their graduate studies at the University of California at Los Angeles and have won awards in national and international competitions. Their project "The Hug" received an honour mention at the Greek Architecture Awards in 2018, and was shortlisted in the top five at the Piranesi Architecture Awards, Piran Slovenia.

In his work, the intention to combine the archetypes of Greek architecture with design ideas that respond to the needs of the 21st century is evident.

Das 2007 von Natasha Deliyianni und Yiorgos Spiridonos gegründete Büro versteht Architektur als Gesamtheit in Zusammenarbeit mit allen Fachbereichen, die das konstruktive und künstlerische Schaffen ergänzen. Das Büro untersucht kleine und große Projekte, sowohl im öffentlichen als auch im privaten Bereich.

Beide Partner haben ihr Studium an der University of California in Los Angeles absolviert und sind Preisträger nationaler und internationaler Wettbewerbe. Ihr Projekt „The Hug" wurde bei den griechischen Architekturpreisen 2018 mit einer lobenden Erwähnung ausgezeichnet und bei den Piranesi Architecture Awards in Piran, Slowenien, in die Vorauswahl der fünf Besten aufgenommen.

In seinem Werk wird die Absicht deutlich, die Archetypen der griechischen Architektur mit Designideen zu verbinden, die den Bedürfnissen des 21. Jahrhunderts entsprechen.

Le cabinet fondé par Natasha Deliyianni et Yiorgos Spiridonos en 2007, conçoit l'architecture comme une totalité en collaboration avec toutes les spécialités qui complètent la création constructive et artistique. Le bureau étudie des projets à petite et grande échelle, tant publics que privés.

Les deux partenaires ont terminé leurs études supérieures à l'Université de Californie à Los Angeles et ont remporté des prix dans des concours nationaux et internationaux. Leur projet « The Hug » a reçu une mention honorable aux Greek Architecture Awards en 2018, et a été présélectionné dans le top 5 des Piranesi Architecture Awards, Piran Slovénie.

Dans son travail, l'intention de combiner les archétypes de l'architecture grecque avec des idées de conception qui répondent aux besoins du 21e siècle est évidente.

La firma fundada por Natasha Deliyianni y Yiorgos Spiridonos en 2007, concibe a la arquitectura como una totalidad en colaboración con todas las especialidades que complementan la creación constructiva y artística. La oficina estudia proyectos de pequeña y gran escala, tanto públicos como privados.

Ambos socios completaron sus estudios de postgrado en la Universidad de California en Los Ángeles y han ganado premios en concursos nacionales e internacionales. Su proyecto «The Hug» recibió una mención de honor en los premios de arquitectura griegos en 2018, y fue pre seleccionado entre los cinco mejores en los premios de arquitectura Piranesi Awards, Piran Eslovenia.

En su trabajo es evidente la intención de combinar los arquetipos de la arquitectura griega con ideas de diseño que respondan a las necesidades del siglo XXI.

REACT ARCHITECTS

NATASHA DELIYIANNI, YIORGOS SPIRIDONOS

ATHENS, GREECE
WWW.RE-ACT.GR

MAISON KAMARI

PAROS ISLAND, GREECE

Photos © Damien De Medeiros

The house stands on a plateau on Kamari, the island of Paros. The contours of the house, which overlooks the mountains and the Aegean Sea, are aligned with the view and create courtyards coupled with a natural slope. The main building is broken down into smaller ones, adapted to the terrain. In this way, the construction is smoothly adjusted and the volume of the house is integrated into the landscape.

The configuration of the openings is associated with the architectural style of the building. Their repetition and likeness dominates the design leaving the white volumes almost untouched.

In the interior, the emphasis is on natural construction materials and finishes. Exposed concrete ceilings, industrial floors and white wood create a cosy and relaxing atmosphere.

The architects selected the furnishings and décor in conjunction with the owners, a couple of film professionals. Period objects were chosen, but also designer pieces in order to create an aesthetic bridge with the architecture.

Das Haus steht auf einem Plateau in Kamari auf der Insel Paros. Die Konturen des Hauses, das auf die Berge und das Ägäische Meer blickt, sind auf die Aussicht ausgerichtet und bilden Innenhöfe in Verbindung mit einem natürlichen Gefälle.

Das Hauptgebäude ist in kleinere, dem Gelände angepasste Gebäude unterteilt. Auf diese Weise wird die Konstruktion reibungslos angepasst und das Volumen des Hauses in die Landschaft integriert.

Die Anordnung der Öffnungen steht im Zusammenhang mit dem architektonischen Stil des Gebäudes. Ihre Wiederholung und Standardisierung dominiert das Design und lässt die weißen Volumen fast unberührt.

Bei der Innenausstattung liegt der Schwerpunkt auf natürlichen Baumaterialien und Oberflächen. Sichtbetondecken, Industrieböden und weißes Holz schaffen eine gemütliche und entspannte Atmosphäre.

Die Architekten wählten die Einrichtung und das Dekor in Zusammenarbeit mit den Eigentümern, einem Ehepaar aus der Filmbranche, aus. Es wurden historische Objekte, aber auch Designerstücke ausgewählt, um eine ästhetische Brücke zur Architektur zu schlagen.

La maison se trouve sur un plateau à Kamari, sur l'île de Paros. Les contours de la maison, qui surplombe les montagnes et la mer Égée, sont alignés sur la vue et créent des cours couplées à une pente naturelle.

Le bâtiment principal est divisé en plusieurs bâtiments plus petits, adaptés au terrain. De cette manière, la construction est ajustée en douceur et le volume de la maison est intégré dans le paysage.

La configuration des ouvertures est associée au style architectural du bâtiment. Leur répétition et leur standardisation dominent le design et laissent les volumes blancs presque intacts.

À l'intérieur, l'accent est mis sur les matériaux de construction et les finitions naturelles. Les plafonds en béton apparent, les sols industriels et le bois blanc créent une atmosphère chaleureuse et relaxante.

Les architectes ont choisi le mobilier et le décor en collaboration avec les propriétaires, un couple de professionnels du cinéma. Des objets d'époque ont été choisis, mais aussi des pièces de design afin de créer un pont esthétique avec l'architecture.

La casa se extiende sobre una meseta en Kamari, la isla de Paros. Los contornos de la vivienda desde la que se ve las montañas y el mar Egeo, se alinean con la vista y crean unos patios acoplados a una pendiente natural.

El edificio principal se descompone en otros más pequeños, adaptados al terreno. De este modo, la construcción se va ajustando suavemente y el volumen de la vivienda queda integrado al paisaje

La configuración de las aberturas se asocia al estilo arquitectónico del edificio. Su repetición y estandarización domina el diseño y deja los volúmenes blancos casi intactos.

En el interior se ha dado protagonismo a los materiales de construcción y los acabados naturales. Los techos de hormigón visto, los suelos industriales y la madera en color blanco crean un ambiente acogedor y relajante.

Los arquitectos seleccionaron el mobiliario y la decoración en forma conjunta con los propietarios, una pareja de profesionales del cine. Se eligieron objetos de época, pero también piezas de diseño con el fin de crear un puente estético con la arquitectura.

Elevations

Sections

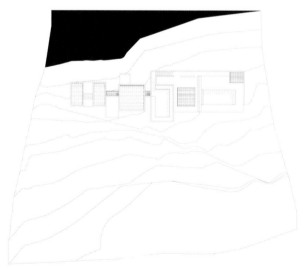

Floor plan

Founded in 2020, Sofía Oliva Arquitectura is an architecture and interior design studio with extensive experience both nationally and internationally. It is characterised by wood construction and the use of natural materials.

SO Arquitectura's aim is to provide architecture and interior design that transcends the traditional. Its philosophy and work is based on a comfortable and sustainable minimalism, which seeks to provide its clients with the greatest happiness. The studio is based in Madrid, and develops projects from the structure and distribution of space, the choice of materials, and the design of furniture and decorative elements.

Sofía Oliva Arquitectura wurde 2020 gegründet und ist ein architektur- und innenarchitekturbüro mit umfassender erfahrung auf nationaler und internationaler ebene. Es zeichnet sich durch holzbauweise und die verwendung natürlicher materialien aus.

Das ziel von SO Arquitectura ist es, architektur und innenarchitektur zu bieten, die über das traditionelle hinausgeht. Ihre philosophie und ihre arbeit basieren auf einem komfortablen und nachhaltigen minimalismus, der darauf abzielt, ihren kunden das größte glück zu bieten. Das studio hat seinen sitz in Madrid und entwickelt projekte, die von der struktur und aufteilung des raums über die wahl der materialien bis hin zum design von möbeln und dekorativen elementen reichen.

Fondé en 2020, Sofía Oliva Arquitectura est un studio d'architecture et de design d'intérieur doté d'une vaste expérience à l'échelle nationale et internationale. Elle se caractérise par une construction en bois et l'utilisation de matériaux naturels.

L'objectif de SO Arquitectura est de proposer une architecture et une décoration intérieure qui transcendent les traditions. Sa philosophie et son travail sont fondés sur un minimalisme confortable et durable, qui vise à procurer le plus grand bonheur à ses clients. Le studio est basé à Madrid, et développe des projets à partir de la structure et de la distribution de l'espace, du choix des matériaux, et du design des meubles et des éléments décoratifs.

Fundado en 2020, Sofía Oliva Arquitectura es un estudio de arquitectura e interiorismo con amplia experiencia en el ámbito nacional e internacional. Se caracteriza por la construcción en madera y el uso de materiales naturales.

El objetivo de SO Arquitectura es proporcionar una arquitectura y un interiorismo que trasciende lo tradicional. Su filosofía y su trabajo se sustenta sobre un minimalismo confortable y sostenible, que busca proporcionar a sus clientes la mayor felicidad. El estudio tiene su sede en Madrid, y desarrolla proyectos desde la estructura y la distribución del espacio, la elección de materiales, y el diseño de mobiliario y elementos decorativos.

SO ARCHITECTURE

SOFIA OLIVA

MADRID, SPAIN
WWW.SOFIAOLIVA.COM

BLANK CANVAS

MADRID, SPAIN

Photos © Javier de Paz, Nacho Uribe Salazar

This flat has been designed for the prestigious Casa Decor interior design show that takes place every year in Madrid. Under Mies van der Rohe's maxim of "less is more", the architect has configured this 22 m² blank canvas with natural materials such as wood, ceramics and linen.

The project is a comfortable minimalist space that combines the modern with the classic, following the guidelines of sustainability. For its configuration, Sofía Oliva has based herself on the union between man and nature applied to the creation of her spaces, which promotes Feng Shui.

White is the main protagonist, this colour and its nuances predominate throughout the space to reinforce the light. But it is also the source of a play of textures and surfaces in the finishes of the walls and furniture.

Diese Wohnung wurde für die prestigeträchtige inneneinrichtungsmesse Casa Decor entworfen, die jedes jahr in Madrid stattfindet. Nach der maxime von Mies van der Rohe „weniger ist mehr" hat der architekt diese 22 m² große leere leinwand mit natürlichen materialien wie holz, keramik und leinen gestaltet.

Das projekt ist ein komfortabler, minimalistischer raum, der das moderne mit dem klassischen verbindet und den richtlinien der nachhaltigkeit folgt. Bei der gestaltung ihrer räume hat sich Sofía Oliva auf die verbindung zwischen mensch und natur gestützt, was dem Feng Shui zugute kommt.

Weiß ist der hauptdarsteller, diese farbe und ihre nuancen überwiegen im gesamten raum und verstärken das licht. Sie ist aber auch die quelle für ein spiel von texturen und oberflächen in den oberflächen der wände und möbel.

Cet appartement a été conçu pour le prestigieux salon de décoration intérieure Casa Decor qui a lieu chaque année à Madrid. Selon la maxime de Mies van der Rohe « moins c'est plus », l'architecte a configuré cette toile blanche de 22 m² avec des matériaux naturels tels que le bois, la céramique et le lin.

Le projet est un espace minimaliste confortable qui combine le moderne et le classique, en suivant les directives de la durabilité. Pour sa configuration, Sofía Oliva s'est basée sur l'union entre l'homme et la nature appliquée à la création de ses espaces, ce qui favorise le Feng Shui.

Le blanc est le principal protagoniste, cette couleur et ses nuances prédominent dans tout l'espace pour renforcer la lumière. Mais c'est aussi la source d'un jeu de textures et de surfaces dans les finitions des murs et des meubles.

Este apartamento ha sido diseñado para la prestigiosa muestra de interiorismo Casa Decor que se realiza cada año en Madrid. Bajo la máxima de Mies van der Rohe del «menos es más», la arquitecta ha configurado este Lienzo en Blanco de 22 m² con materiales naturales como la madera, la cerámica y el lino.

El proyecto es un espacio minimalista confortable que combina lo moderno con lo clásico siguiendo las pautas de la sostenibilidad. Para su configuración, Sofía Oliva se ha basado en la unión entre el hombre y la naturaleza aplicada a la creación de sus espacios, que promueve el Feng Shui.

El blanco es el gran protagonista, este color y sus matices predomina en todo el espacio para reforzar la luz. Pero también es fuente de juego de texturas y superficies en los acabados de las paredes y el mobiliario.

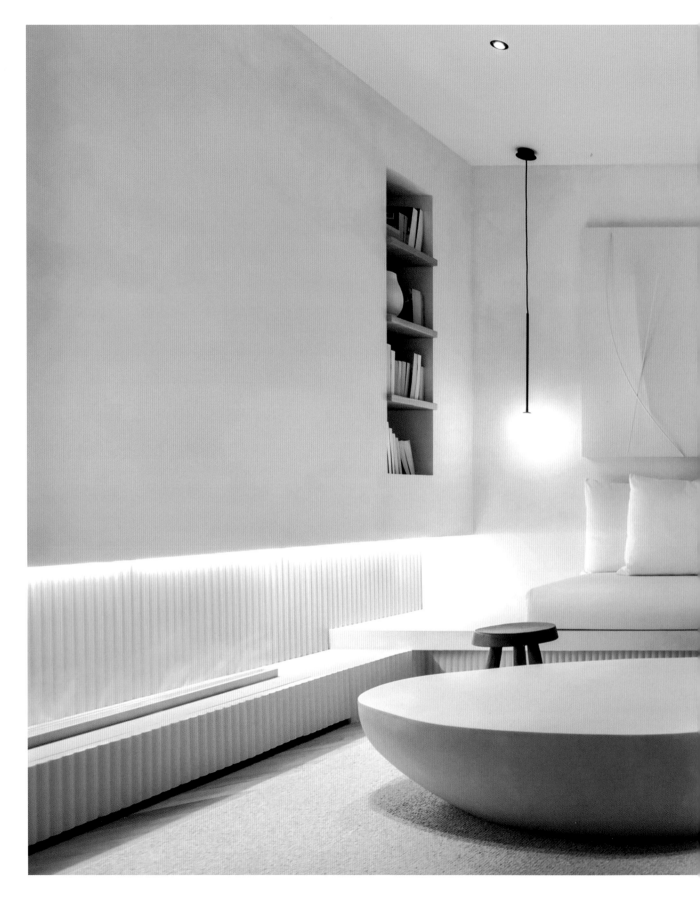

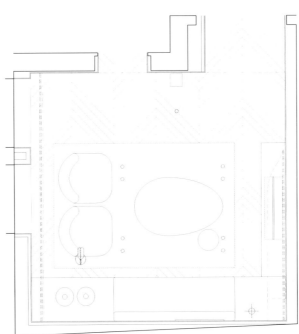

Floor plan

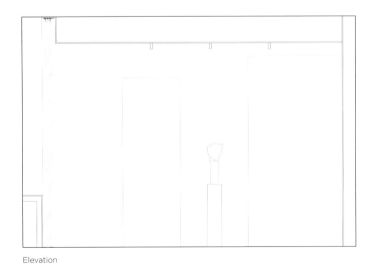

Elevation

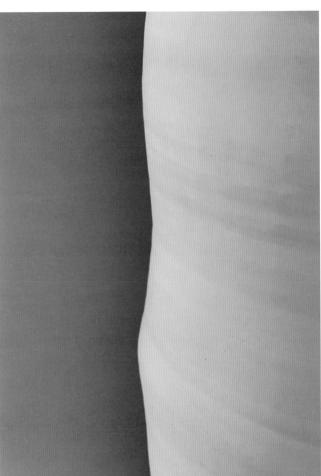

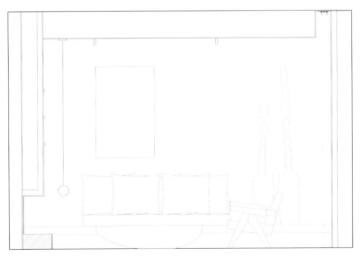

Elevation

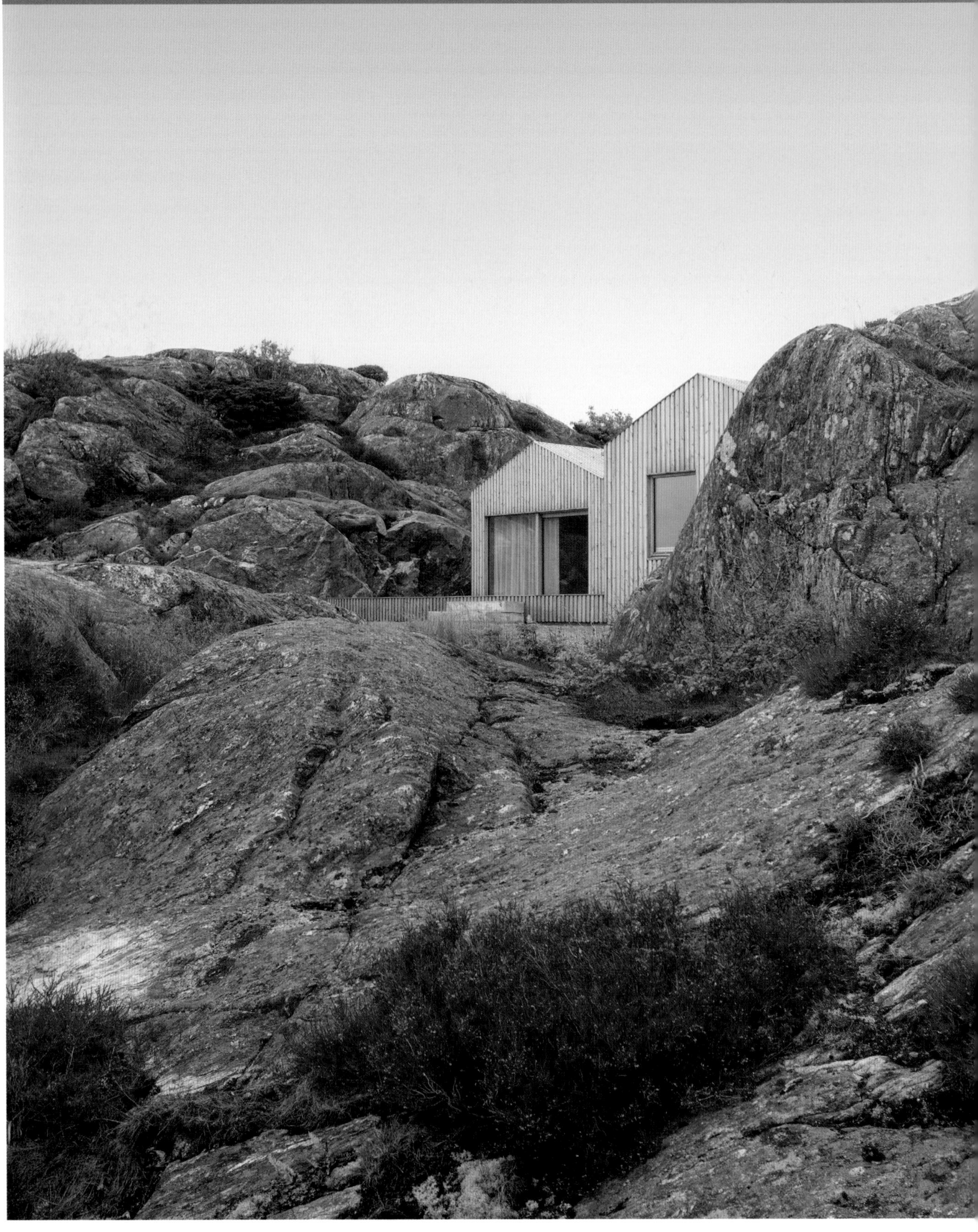

Founded by Mathias Holmberg in 2018, Studio Holmberg focuses on exploratory architecture and small-scale installations, including private residences, home extensions and flat refurbishments. The Gothenburg-based firm approaches each project holistically, from volume, materials, and details, to interior design and furnishings. Studio Holmberg seeks to combine geographical and historical knowledge of the sites with innovative practical solutions. Projects are designed with consideration for local traditions and harmony with the surrounding nature. The studio combines drawing, design and carpentry on site, to deepen the knowledge of the materials and the site, and allow the project to evolve. Mathias Holmberg holds a master's degree in architecture and urban design from Chalmers University of Technology. Between 2011 and 2018 he worked in architecture offices in Stockholm, Copenhagen and Gothenburg.

Das 2018 von Mathias Holmberg gegründete Studio Holmberg konzentriert sich auf experimentelle Architektur und kleine Installationen, darunter Privatwohnungen, Hauserweiterungen und Wohnungsrenovierungen. Das in Göteborg ansässige Unternehmen geht an jedes Projekt ganzheitlich heran, von Volumen, Materialien und Details bis hin zu Inneneinrichtung und Möblierung. Das Studio Holmberg ist bestrebt, geografische und historische Kenntnisse der Orte mit innovativen praktischen Lösungen zu verbinden. Die Projekte werden unter Berücksichtigung lokaler Traditionen und im Einklang mit der umgebenden Natur entworfen. Das Studio kombiniert Zeichnung, Entwurf und Tischlerei vor Ort, um die Kenntnis der Materialien und des Ortes zu vertiefen und das Projekt weiterzuentwickeln. Mathias Holmberg hat einen Master-Abschluss in Architektur und Stadtplanung von der Chalmers University of Technology. Zwischen 2011 und 2018 arbeitete er in Architekturbüros in Stockholm, Kopenhagen und Göteborg.

Fondé par Mathias Holmberg en 2018, le Studio Holmberg se concentre sur l'architecture exploratoire et les installations à petite échelle, notamment les résidences privées, les extensions de maisons et les réaménagements d'appartements. L'entreprise basée à Göteborg aborde chaque projet de manière holistique, du volume, des matériaux et des détails à l'aménagement intérieur et à l'ameublement. Le Studio Holmberg cherche à combiner la connaissance géographique et historique des sites avec des solutions pratiques innovantes. Les projets sont conçus en tenant compte des traditions locales et en harmonie avec la nature environnante. L'atelier combine le dessin, la conception et la menuiserie sur place, pour approfondir la connaissance des matériaux et du site, et permettre au projet d'évoluer. Mathias Holmberg est titulaire d'une maîtrise en architecture et en design urbain de l'université de technologie de Chalmers. Entre 2011 et 2018, il a travaillé dans des bureaux d'architecture à Stockholm, Copenhague et Göteborg.

Fundado por Mathias Holmberg en 2018, Studio Holmberg se centra en la arquitectura exploratoria y en las instalaciones a pequeña escala, incluyendo residencias privadas, ampliaciones de viviendas y reformas de apartamentos. La firma con sede en Gotemburgo aborda cada proyecto de manera integral, desde el volumen, los materiales, y los detalles, hasta el diseño de interiores y el mobiliario. Studio Holmberg busca combinar el conocimiento geográfico e histórico de los emplazamientos, con soluciones prácticas innovadoras. Los proyectos se diseñan teniendo en cuenta las tradiciones locales y la armonía con la naturaleza circundante. El estudio combina el dibujo, el diseño y la carpintería in situ, para profundizar el conocimiento de los materiales y el lugar, y permitir que el proyecto evolucione. Mathias Holmberg tiene un master en arquitectura y diseño urbano de la Universidad Tecnológica de Chalmers. Entre 2011 y 2018 trabajó en oficinas de arquitectura en Estocolmo, Copenhague y Gotemburgo.

STUDIO HOLMBERG

MATHIAS HOLMBERG

GOTHENBURG, SWEDEN
WWW.STUDIOHOLMBERG.SE

VILLA VASSDAL

GOTHENBURG, SWEDEN

Photos © Markus Bülow

This summer house is a minimalist counterpoint to the rocky enclave of a small island in the Gothenburg archipelago. With a low profile, and shifting, fragmented volumes, the house replicates the characteristics and scale of the area.

All façades and roofs are clad in untreated pinewood. Over time, the finish will turn grey, with the house blending more and more into its surroundings of exposed cliffs and barren vegetation. The division and displacement of the volumes create weather-protected and secluded areas that act as terraces and courtyards. Each body of the house marks a change of function: bedrooms, living area, kitchen, toilets. The orientation of the interior spaces offers privacy and protection from the sun, but maintains a close relationship with the exterior.

Moving through the house offers a choreographed experience with changing sight lines, culminating in a view towards the sea. The same solidity that the exterior conveys continues in the interior areas where the walls and ceilings are clad in birch plywood.

Dieses Sommerhaus bildet einen minimalistischen Kontrapunkt zur felsigen Enklave einer kleinen Insel im Göteborger Schärengarten. Mit seinem niedrigen Profil und den sich verschiebenden, fragmentierten Volumina nimmt das Haus die Merkmale und den Maßstab der Gegend auf.

Alle Fassaden und Dächer sind mit unbehandeltem Kiefernholz verkleidet. Mit der Zeit vergraut der Anstrich und das Haus fügt sich mehr und mehr in die Umgebung mit ihren exponierten Felsen und der kargen Vegetation ein. Durch die Teilung und Verschiebung der Volumen entstehen wettergeschützte und geschützte Bereiche, die als Terrassen und Höfe fungieren. Jeder Teil des Hauses hat eine andere Funktion: Schlafzimmer, Wohnbereich, Küche, Toilette. Die Ausrichtung der Innenräume bietet Privatsphäre und Schutz vor der Sonne, stellt aber gleichzeitig eine enge Verbindung zum Außenbereich her.

Die Bewegung durch das Haus bietet eine choreografierte Erfahrung mit wechselnden Sichtachsen, die in einem Blick auf das Meer gipfelt. Die gleiche Solidität, die das Äußere vermittelt, setzt sich in den Innenräumen fort, wo die Wände und Decken mit Birkensperrholz verkleidet sind.

Cette maison d'été est un contrepoint minimaliste à l'enclave rocheuse d'une petite île de l'archipel de Göteborg. Avec un profil bas, et des volumes changeants et fragmentés, la maison reproduit les caractéristiques et l'échelle de la zone.

Toutes les façades et les toits sont revêtus de bois de pin non traité. Avec le temps, la finition deviendra grise et la maison se fondra de plus en plus dans son environnement de falaises exposées et de végétation stérile. La division et le déplacement des volumes créent des zones protégées des intempéries et isolées qui font office de terrasses et de cours. Chaque corps de la maison marque un changement de fonction : chambres, salon, cuisine, toilettes. L'orientation des espaces intérieurs offre intimité et protection contre le soleil, mais maintient une relation étroite avec l'extérieur.

Se déplacer dans la maison offre une expérience chorégraphiée avec des lignes de vue changeantes, qui culmine avec une vue sur la mer. La solidité de l'extérieur se retrouve à l'intérieur, où les murs et les plafonds sont recouverts de contreplaqué de bouleau.

Esta casa de verano es un contrapunto minimalista al enclave rocoso de una pequeña isla en el archipiélago de Gotemburgo. Con un perfil bajo, y volúmenes cambiantes y fragmentados, la vivienda replica las características y la escala de la zona.

Todas las fachadas y tejados tienen un revestimiento de madera de pino sin tratar. Con el tiempo, el acabado se irá volviendo gris y hará que la casa se funda cada vez más con su entorno de acantilados expuestos y vegetación estéril. La división y el desplazamiento de los volúmenes crean zonas protegidas de la intemperie y aislados que actúan como terrazas y patios. Cada cuerpo de la vivienda marca un cambio de función: dormitorios, zona de estar, cocina, lavabos. La orientación de los espacios interiores ofrece privacidad y protege del sol, pero mantienen una relación estrecha con el exterior.

Moverse por la casa ofrece una experiencia coreografiada con líneas de visión cambiantes, que culmina con una vista hacia el mar. La misma solidez que transmite el exterior continúa en las zonas interiores donde las paredes y los techos están revestidos de contrachapado de abedul.

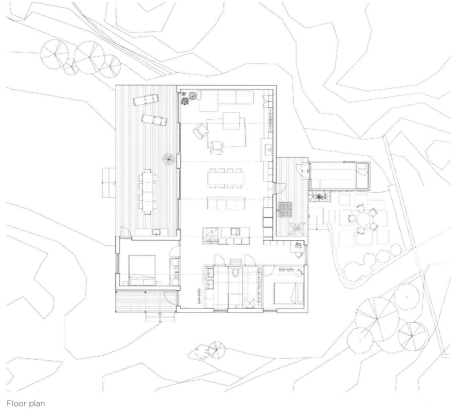

Floor plan

Studio Wet is an architecture, landscape and urban design firm. Its founders, Jose Gómez Mora and Daniel Montes Estrada are graduates of the University of Seville and have international experience in offices in the UK and Switzerland. Their track record reflects a diverse range of projects based on a strong contemporary design, open to collaboration and interdisciplinary work. Studio Wet architects have shared their experiences at conferences at several Spanish universities. In addition, they received the award for best residential building from the Institute of Architects of Seville (2019) for the Lissen House and recently the award for best building at national level from the same Institute for the Borrero House. Their work is based on what they call "critical pragmatism", that is, an acceptance of the contingencies of the conditioning factors of the project in order to achieve, in an optimistic way, the most radical and at the same time the most appropriate contemporary proposal.

Studio Wet ist ein Architektur-, Landschafts- und Stadtplanungsbüro. Die Gründer, Jose Gómez Mora und Daniel Montes Estrada, sind Absolventen der Universität Sevilla und verfügen über internationale Erfahrung in Büros in Großbritannien und der Schweiz. Ihre Erfolgsbilanz spiegelt eine breite Palette von Projekten wider, die auf einem starken zeitgenössischen Design basieren und offen für Zusammenarbeit und interdisziplinäre Arbeit sind. Die Architekten von Studio Wet haben ihre Erfahrungen auf Konferenzen an mehreren spanischen Universitäten mitgeteilt. Darüber hinaus erhielten sie den Preis für das beste Wohngebäude der Architektenkammer von Sevilla (2019) für das Haus Lissen und kürzlich den Preis für das beste Gebäude auf nationaler Ebene von derselben Kammer für das Haus Borrero. Ihre Arbeit basiert auf dem, was sie als „kritischen Pragmatismus" bezeichnen, d.h. auf der Akzeptanz der Unwägbarkeiten der das Projekt bedingenden Faktoren, um auf optimistische Weise den radikalsten und gleichzeitig angemessensten zeitgenössischen Vorschlag zu erreichen.

Le Studio Wet est un cabinet d'architecture, de paysage et de design urbain. Ses fondateurs, Jose Gómez Mora et Daniel Montes Estrada, sont diplômés de l'université de Séville et ont une expérience internationale dans des bureaux au Royaume-Uni et en Suisse. Leurs antécédents reflètent une gamme variée de projets basés sur un design contemporain fort, ouvert à la collaboration et au travail interdisciplinaire. Les architectes du Studio Wet ont partagé leurs expériences lors de conférences dans plusieurs universités espagnoles. En outre, ils ont reçu le prix du meilleur bâtiment résidentiel de l'Association des Architectes de Séville (2019) pour la maison Lissen et récemment le prix du meilleur bâtiment au niveau national du même Association pour la maison Borrero. Leur travail est basé sur ce qu'ils appellent le « pragmatisme critique », c'est-à-dire l'acceptation des contingences des facteurs conditionnant le projet afin de parvenir, de manière optimiste, à la proposition contemporaine la plus radicale et en même temps la plus appropriée.

Studio Wet es una firma de arquitectura, paisajismo y diseño urbano. Sus fundadores, Jose Gómez Mora y Daniel Montes Estrada son egresados de la Universidad de Sevilla y cuentan con experiencia internacional en despachos del Reino Unido y Suiza. Su trayectoria refleja una diversa gama de proyectos basados en un marcado diseño contemporáneo, abierto a la colaboración y al trabajo interdisciplinar. Los arquitectos de Studio Wet han compartido sus experiencias en conferencias en varias universidades españolas. Además, recibieron el premio a mejor edificio residencial del Colegio de Arquitectos de Sevilla (2019) por la Casa Lissen y recientemente el premio a mejor edificio nivel nacional del mismo Colegio por la Casa Borrero. Su trabajo parte de lo que ellos denominan «pragmatismo crítico», esto es una aceptación de las contingencias de los condicionantes del proyecto para conseguir de una manera optimista, la propuesta contemporánea más radical y a la vez más adecuada.

STUDIO WET

DANIEL MONTES ESTRADA, JOSE GÓMEZ MORA

SEVILLE, SPAIN
WWW.STUDIOWET.COM

BORRERO HOUSE

HUELVA, SPAIN

Photos © Fernando Alda

In Alosno, a small village in Huelva known for its fandangos and Iberian pork products, its proximity to the Tharsis mines and its English architecture, the architects were commissioned to build a village house on a plot with a frontage of 7 m and a depth of 40. This archetypal house was built using a traditional system: load-bearing walls in bays parallel to the façade. But the architects took advantage of the great depth of the plot to make the elongated headwall the new main façade. So the house was built on one floor, with a single bay and a single slope along these 40 m. The rooms of the house are aligned with the new façade and are separated from the garage by a large courtyard that serves as an entrance. In this way, the programme does not break the unity of the volume. In the same spirit, the outer face of the façade load-bearing wall is curved rhythmically to better support, both aesthetically and statically, the large sloping flat tile roof. Two types of brick are alternated, one rectangular and the other with a curved corner, in order to blur the wall effect of a 40 m long wall.

In Alosno, einem kleinen Dorf in Huelva, das für seine Fandangos und iberischen Schweinefleischprodukte, seine Nähe zu den Tharsis-Minen und seine englische Architektur bekannt ist, wurden die Architekten beauftragt, ein Dorfhaus auf einem Grundstück mit einer Front von sieben Metern und einer Tiefe von vierzig Metern zu bauen. Dieses archetypische Haus wurde nach einem traditionellen System gebaut: tragende Wände in parallel zur Fassade verlaufenden Erkern. Doch die Architekten nutzten die große Tiefe des Grundstücks, um die langgestreckte Wand zur neuen Hauptfassade zu machen. Das Haus wurde also auf einer Ebene gebaut, mit einem einzigen Erker und einer einzigen Schräge auf einer Länge von 40 m. Die Räume des Hauses orientieren sich an der neuen Fassade und sind durch einen großen Hof, der als Eingang dient, von der Garage getrennt. Auf diese Weise unterbricht das Programm nicht die Einheit des Bandes. In diesem Sinne ist auch die Außenwand der tragenden Fassade rhythmisch gebogen, um das große geneigte Flachdach aus Ziegeln sowohl ästhetisch als auch statisch besser zu unterstützen. Zwei Arten von Ziegeln, ein rechteckiger und ein gebogener, werden abwechselnd verwendet, um die Mauerwirkung einer 40 Meter langen Wand zu verwischen.

À Alosno, petit village de Huelva connu pour ses fandangos et ses produits de porc ibérique, sa proximité des mines de Tharsis et son architecture anglaise, les architectes ont été chargés de construire une maison de village sur un terrain de sept mètres de façade et de quarante mètres de profondeur. Cet archétype de maison a été construit selon un système traditionnel : des murs porteurs en travées parallèles à la façade. Mais les architectes ont profité de la grande profondeur du terrain pour faire du mur allongé la nouvelle façade principale. La maison a donc été construite sur un seul niveau, avec une seule baie et une seule pente sur les 40 m de longueur. Les pièces de la maison sont alignées avec la nouvelle façade et sont séparées du garage par une grande cour qui sert d'entrée. De cette manière, le programme ne rompt pas l'unité du volume. Dans le même esprit, la face extérieure du mur porteur de la façade est incurvée de façon rythmique pour mieux supporter, tant sur le plan esthétique que statique, la grande toiture inclinée en tuiles plates. Deux types de briques, l'une rectangulaire et l'autre avec un coin incurvé, sont alternés afin d'estomper l'effet de paroi d'un mur de 40 m de long.

En Alosno, un pueblo pequeño de Huelva conocido por sus fandangos y sus chacinas de cerdo ibérico, la cercanía a las minas de Tharsis y su arquitectura inglesa, los arquitectos reciben el encargo para hacer una casa de pueblo en una parcela de siete metros de fachada y cuarenta de profundidad. Esta vivienda arquetípica se construye con un sistema tradicional: muros de carga en crujías paralelas a la fachada. Pero los arquitectos aprovecharon la gran profundidad de la parcela para hacer de la pared alargada, la nueva fachada principal. De manera que se construyó la casa en una planta, con una única crujía y a un agua a lo largo de esos 40 m. Las habitaciones de la vivienda están alineadas a la nueva fachada y se encuentran separadas del garaje por un gran patio que funciona como entrada. De esta manera el programa no rompe la unidad del volumen. Con ese mismo ánimo, la cara exterior del muro de carga de fachada se curva rítmicamente para soportar mejor, tanto estética como estáticamente, la gran cubierta inclinada de teja plana. Así se alterna dos tipos de ladrillo, uno rectangular y otro de esquina curva, para desdibujar el efecto tapia de un paramento de 40 m de longitud.

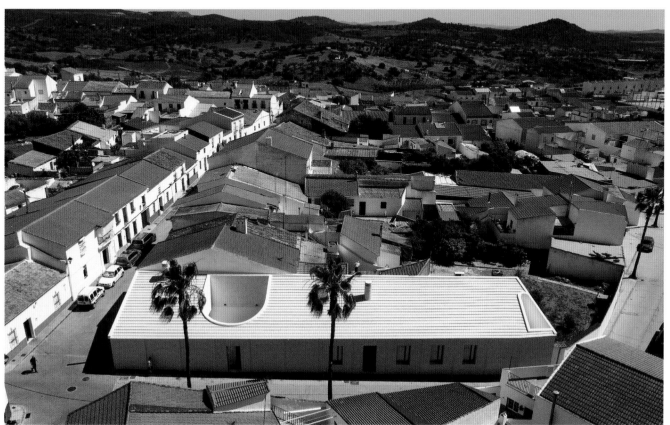

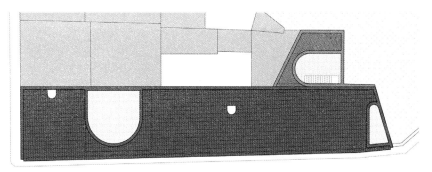

Roof plan

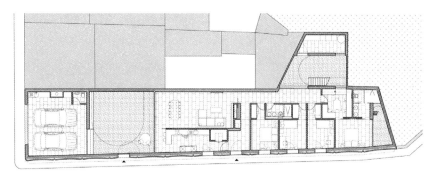

Ground floor plan

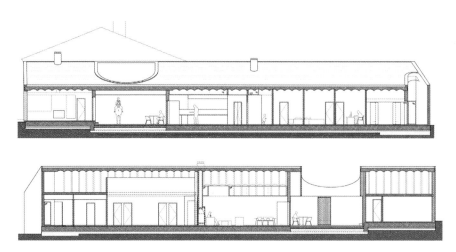

Longitudinal sections

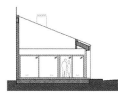

Section through main patio

Section through kitchen

Section through hall

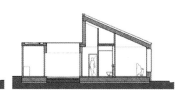

Section through patio and bedrooms

Section through hall

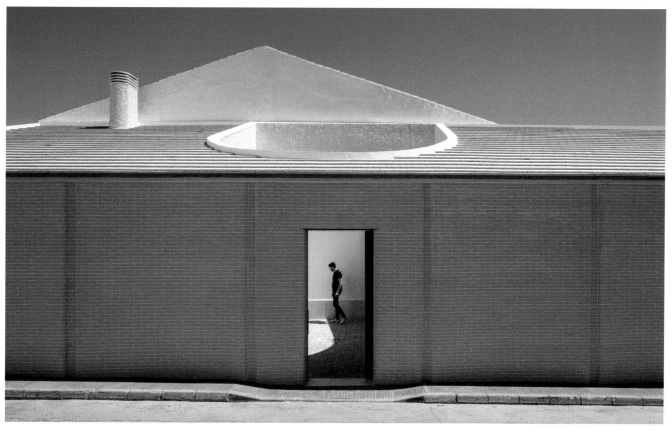

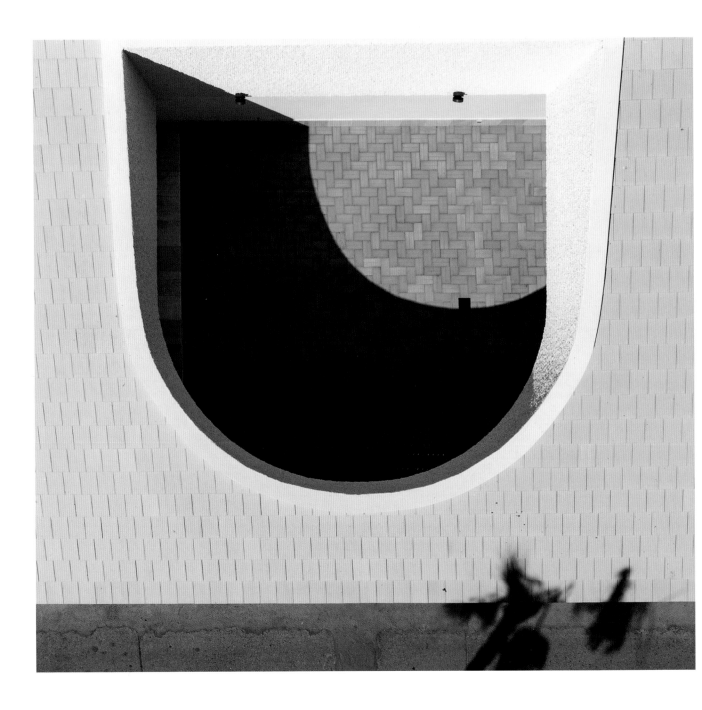

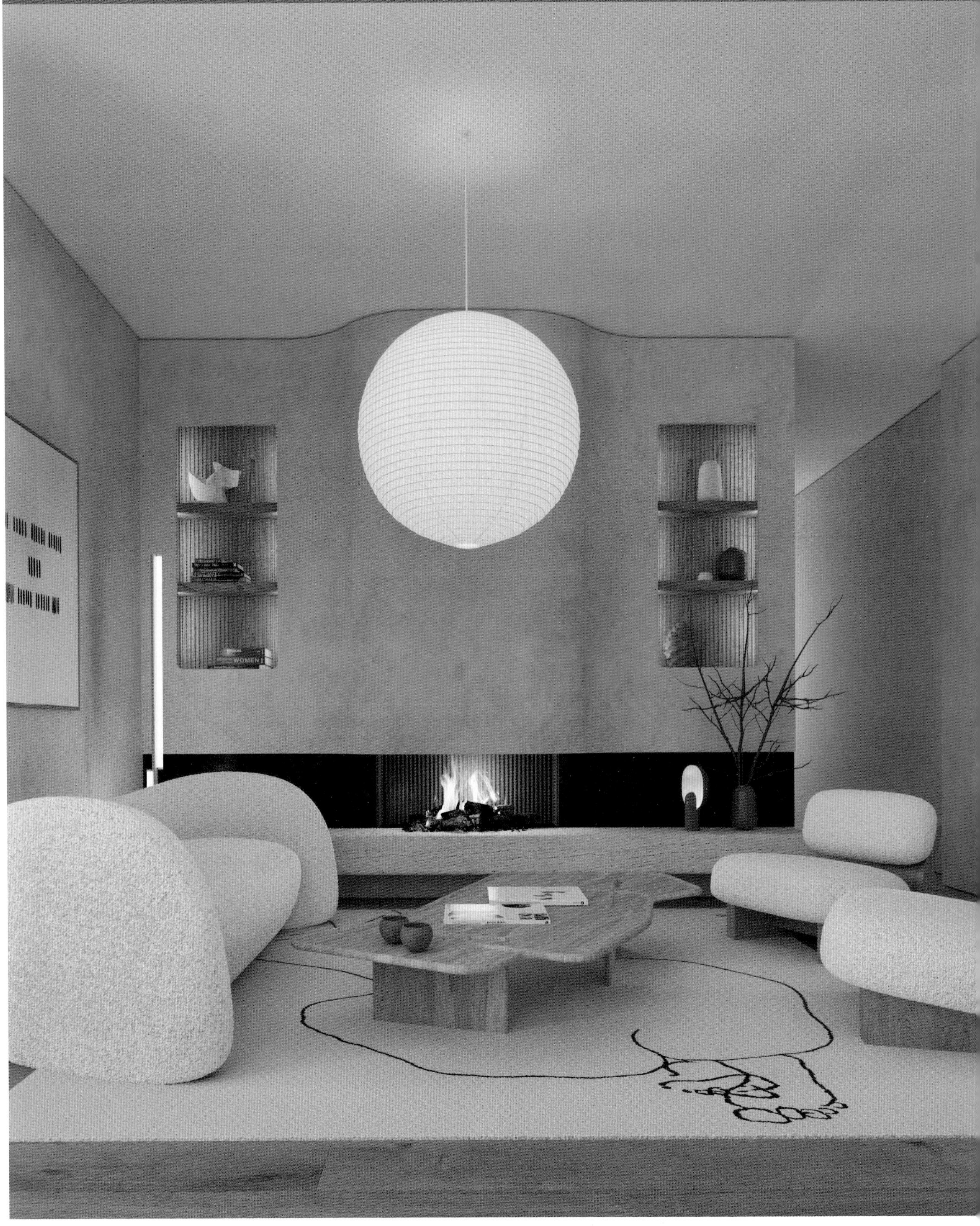

The Room Studio was founded in 2005 in Barcelona by interior designer Meritxell Ribé and architect Josep Puigdomènech, both creative directors. Their work ranges from decorative, architectural and interior design solutions to the construction of works that require special treatment.

The firm's hallmark is warm and welcoming atmospheres. The incorporation of home automation and technology in each of its projects, together with a meticulous study of lighting, make its spaces enjoyable for all five senses.

Since its foundation, The Room Studio has carried out several residential projects, many of which have received distinctions and awards such as Best Project at Casa Decor, Gold Medal at the London Design Awards, Bronze Medal at the International Design Awards (IDA), and Best of 2020 at Archello, among others.

The Room Studio wurde 2005 in Barcelona von der Innenarchitektin Meritxell Ribé und dem Architekten Josep Puigdomènech, beide Kreativdirektoren, gegründet. Ihre Arbeit reicht von dekorativen, architektonischen und innenarchitektonischen Lösungen bis hin zum Bau von Werken, die eine besondere Behandlung erfordern.

Das Markenzeichen der Kanzlei ist eine warme und einladende Atmosphäre. Die Einbindung von Haustechnik und Technologie in jedes ihrer Projekte sowie die sorgfältige Planung der Beleuchtung ermöglichen es, ihre Räume mit allen fünf Sinnen zu genießen.

Seit seiner Gründung hat The Room Studio mehrere wohnprojekte realisiert, von denen viele auszeichnungen und preise erhielten, wie z. B. Best Project bei Casa Decor, Goldmedaille bei den London Design Awards, Bronzemedaille bei den International Design Awards (IDA) und Best of 2020 bei Archello, um nur einige zu nennen.

The Room Studio a été fondé en 2005 à Barcelone par la décoratrice d'intérieur Meritxell Ribé et l'architecte Josep Puigdomènech, tous deux directeurs de la création. Leur travail va des solutions de décoration, d'architecture et d'aménagement intérieur à la construction d'ouvrages nécessitant un traitement spécial.

La marque de fabrique du cabinet est une atmosphère chaleureuse et accueillante. L'incorporation de la domotique et de la technologie dans chacun de ses projets, ainsi qu'une étude minutieuse de l'éclairage, permettent de profiter de ses espaces avec les cinq sens.

Depuis sa fondation, The Room Studio a réalisé de nombreux projets résidentiels, dont beaucoup ont reçu des distinctions et des prix tels que le meilleur projet à Casa Decor, la médaille d'or aux London Design Awards, la médaille de bronze aux International Design Awards (IDA) et le Best of 2020 à Archello, entre autres.

The Room Studio nació en el año 2005 en Barcelona de la mano de la interiorista Meritxell Ribé y el arquitecto Josep Puigdomènech, ambos directores creativos. Su trabajo abarca desde soluciones decorativas, arquitectónicas y de interiorismo, hasta la construcción de obras que requieren un tratamiento especial.

El sello de la firma son las atmósferas cálidas y acogedoras. La incorporación en cada uno de los proyectos de la domótica y la tecnología, junto a un minucioso estudio de la iluminación, hacen que sus espacios se puedan disfrutar con los cinco sentidos.

Desde su fundación, en The Room Studio han llevado a cabo numerosos proyectos residenciales, muchos de los cuales han recibido distinciones y premios como el de mejor proyecto en Casa Decor, Medalla de Oro en London Design Awards, Medalla de Bronce en los International Design Awards (IDA), y el Best of 2020 en Archello, entre otros.

THE ROOM STUDIO

JOSEP PUIGDOMÈNECH, MERITXELL RIBÉ

BARCELONA, SPAIN
WWW.THEROOM-STUDIO.COM

PASEO DE GRACIA

BARCELONA, SPAIN

Photos © The Room Studio

The "Wabi Sabi" concept seeks the beauty of imperfection caused by the passage of time. This interpretation is the basis for this 230 m² flat project. The owner was looking for a timeless space where materials evolve naturally over time. One of the main premises was to create an environment of comfort and avoid the feeling of perfection and coldness.

This flat, located in one of Barcelona's most emblematic streets, had a very separated layout. The connections between the rooms were made through narrow passages that made it difficult to move around smoothly. For this reason, the first objective of the interior design project was to open up these spaces to provide each corner with amplitude and natural light.

Noble materials with neutral and calm tones such as micro-cement, iron and wood infused the home with personality and a minimalist avant-garde style. The decoration project brought warmth and comfort to each area thanks to the selection of furniture, lighting pieces and the use of carpets and textiles. All the elements become the protagonists of each room.

Das „Wabi Sabi"-Konzept sucht nach der Schönheit der Unvollkommenheit, die durch den Lauf der Zeit entsteht. Diese Interpretation bildet die Grundlage für dieses 230 m² große Wohnungsprojekt. Der Eigentümer suchte nach einem zeitlosen Raum, in dem sich die Materialien im Laufe der Zeit natürlich entwickeln. Eine der Hauptprämissen war es, eine komfortable Umgebung zu schaffen und das Gefühl von Perfektion und Kälte zu vermeiden.

Diese Wohnung, die in einer der emblematischsten Straßen Barcelonas liegt, war sehr kleinteilig angelegt. Die Verbindungen zwischen den Zimmern wurden durch enge Gänge hergestellt, die es schwierig machten, sich reibungslos zu bewegen. Aus diesem Grund bestand das erste Ziel des Innenarchitekturprojekts darin, diese Räume zu öffnen, um jede Ecke mit Weite und natürlichem Licht zu versehen.

Edle Materialien in neutralen und ruhigen Tönen wie Mikrozement, Eisen und Holz verleihen dem Haus Persönlichkeit und einen minimalistischen, avantgardistischen Stil. Das Dekorationsprojekt brachte Wärme und Komfort in jeden Bereich dank der Auswahl von Möbeln, Beleuchtungselementen und der Verwendung von Teppichen und Textilien. Alle Elemente werden zu Protagonisten der einzelnen Räume.

Le concept « Wabi Sabi » recherche la beauté de l'imperfection causée par le passage du temps. Cette interprétation est à la base de ce projet d'appartement de 230 m². Le propriétaire était à la recherche d'un espace intemporel où les matériaux évoluent naturellement au fil du temps. L'une des principales prémisses était de créer un environnement de confort et d'éviter le sentiment de perfection et de froideur.

Cet appartement, situé dans l'une des rues les plus emblématiques de Barcelone, avait une disposition très compartimentée. Les liaisons entre les pièces se faisaient par des passages étroits qui rendaient difficile une circulation fluide. Pour cette raison, le premier objectif du projet d'aménagement intérieur a été d'ouvrir ces espaces pour donner à chaque coin de l'amplitude et de la lumière naturelle.

Des matériaux nobles aux tons neutres et calmes tels que le microciment, le fer et le bois ont insufflé à la maison une personnalité et un style minimaliste d'avant-garde. Le projet de décoration a apporté chaleur et confort à chaque espace grâce à la sélection des meubles, des pièces d'éclairage et à l'utilisation de tapis et de textiles. Tous les éléments deviennent les protagonistes de chaque pièce.

El concepto «Wabi Sabi» busca la belleza de la imperfección causada por el paso de los años. Dicha interpretación es la base para este proyecto de un piso de 230 m². El propietario buscaba un espacio atemporal donde los materiales evolucionen de forma natural con el tiempo. Una de las principales premisas era crear un entorno de confort y evitar la sensación de perfección y frialdad.

Este piso situado en una de las calles más emblemáticas de Barcelona, presentaba una distribución muy compartimentada. Las conexiones entre las estancias se daban a través de pasos estrechos que dificultaban un recorrido fluido. Por ello, el primer objetivo del proyecto de interiorismo fue abrir estos espacios para dotar de amplitud y luz natural a cada rincón.

Materiales nobles con tonalidades neutras y sosegadas como el microcemento, el hierro y la madera, infundieron personalidad a la vivienda y un estilo minimalista de vanguardia. El proyecto de decoración permitió aportar calidez y comodidad a cada área gracias a la selección de mobiliario, piezas de iluminación y despliegue de alfombras y textiles. Todos los elementos pasan a ser los protagonistas de cada estancia.

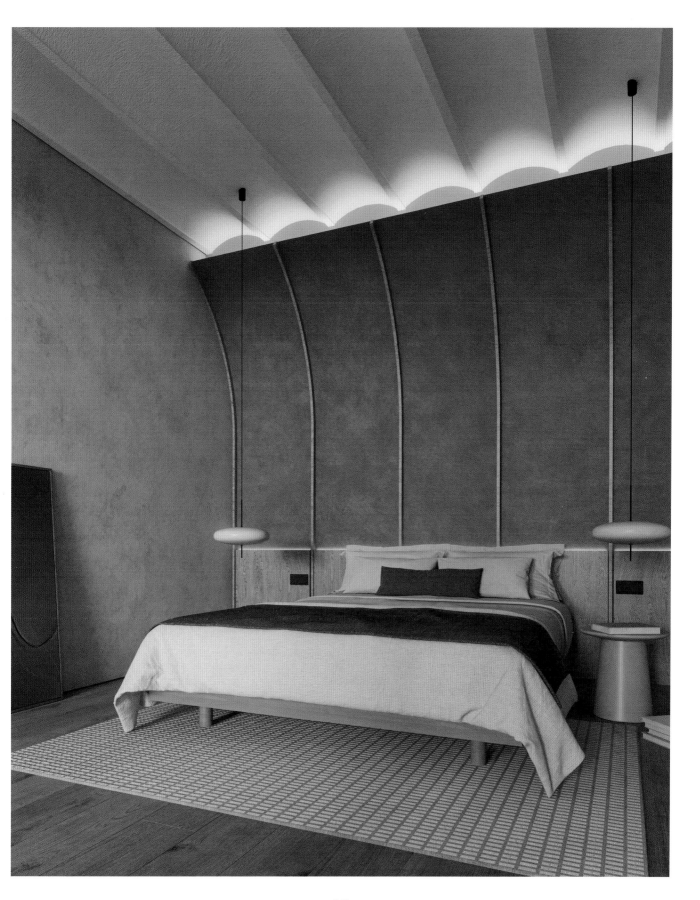

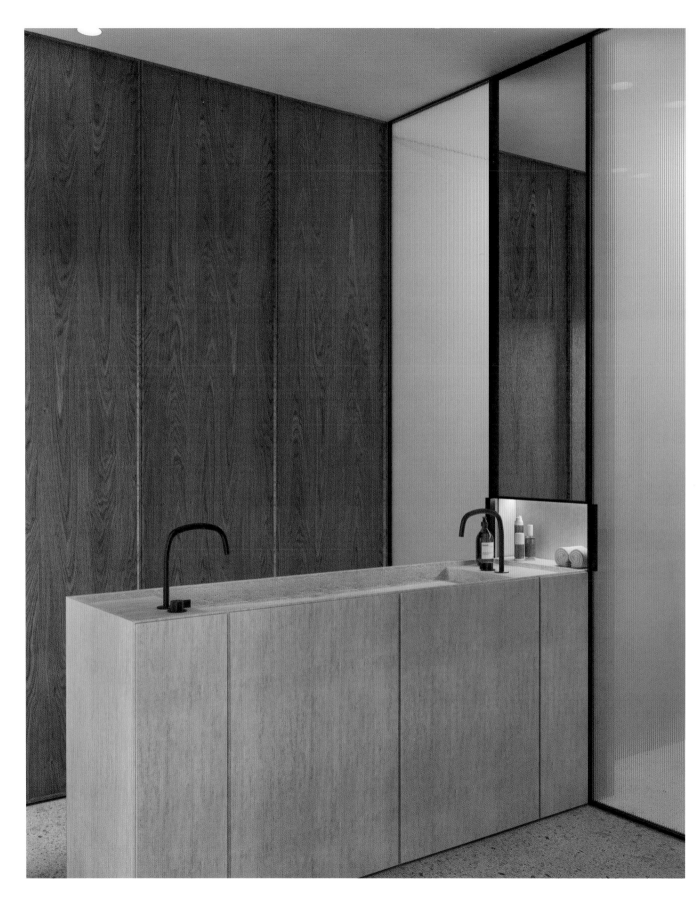

Thaïs Niville studied interior design at the Royal Academy of Fine Arts in Ghent. Before founding her own studio in 2013, she did her intership with Nathalie Deboel, and there she knew that this would be her profession for life. She also worked as a freelance designer for Bieke Casteleyn's atelier and her furniture brand.

Ville Design's interior designs stand out for their good taste, simplicity and the counterpoint of luxury finishes. Their projects are sober and warm at the same time. Natural materials with soft colours, organic shapes and iconic pieces of furniture are the hallmark of their projects.

Thaïs Niville studierte Innenarchitektur an der Königlichen Akademie der Schönen Künste in Gent. Bevor sie 2013 ihr eigenes studio gründete, absolvierte sie ein praktikum bei Nathalie Deboel, und dort wusste sie, dass dies ihr Beruf fürs Leben sein würde. Außerdem arbeitete sie als freiberufliche Designerin für das Atelier von Bieke Casteleyn und ihre Möbelmarke.

Die Inneneinrichtungen von Ville Design zeichnen sich durch ihren guten Geschmack, ihre Schlichtheit und den Kontrapunkt der luxuriösen Ausstattungen aus. Ihre Projekte sind nüchtern und warm zugleich. Natürliche Materialien mit sanften Farben, organische Formen und ikonische Möbelstücke sind das Markenzeichen ihrer Projekte.

Thaïs Niville a étudié la décoration d'intérieur à l'Académie royale des Beaux-Arts de Gand. Avant de fonder son propre studio en 2013, elle a fait son stage avec Nathalie Deboel, et là, elle a su que ce serait son métier pour la vie. Elle a également travaillé en tant que designer indépendante pour l'atelier de Bieke Casteleyn et sa marque de meubles.

Les aménagements intérieurs de Ville Design se distinguent par leur bon goût, leur simplicité et le contrepoint de finitions luxueuses. Leurs projets sont à la fois sobres et chaleureux. Les matériaux naturels aux couleurs douces, les formes organiques et les pièces de mobilier emblématiques sont la marque de fabrique de leurs projets.

Thaïs Niville estudió diseño de interiores en la Real Academia de Bellas Artes de Gante. Antes de fundar su estudio propio en el año 2013, hizo sus prácticas con Nathalie Deboel, y allí supo que ésta sería su profesión de por vida. También realizó colaboraciones como diseñadora autónoma para el atelier de Bieke Casteleyn y su marca de mobiliario.

Los interiorismos de Ville Design destacan por el buen gusto, la sencillez y el contrapunto de los acabados de lujo. Sus proyectos son sobrios y cálidos a la vez. Materiales naturales con colores suaves, formas orgánicas y piezas de mobiliario icónicas son el sello definitivo de sus proyectos.

VILLE DESIGN

THAÏS NIVILLE

GHENT, BELGIUM
WWW.VILLEDESIGN.BE

VPS RÉSIDENCE

OUDENAARDE, BELGIUM

Photos © Thomas De Bruyne - Cafeine

The owners wanted a house to take refuge from the hustle and bustle, an important guideline for people who lived in the countryside and moved to the city. Familiar with the language of design through their own furniture shop, Angelique Segaert, they contacted Thaïs Niville and the affinity was immediate.

To give the timeless air that the clients were looking for, the designer chose exclusive pieces of furniture that stand the test of time, such as the Pierre Jeanneret chairs, the Edifice lamp by Elisa Uberti and the "The line" table by Nathalie Deboel. The finishes are dominated by natural materials such as stone, oak wood for the floor and tadelakt in the bathroom. The textiles in strict white or neutral colours create a contrast of warmth: wool rugs and floor-to-ceiling linen curtains filter the light that enters through the large windows throughout the house. In the kitchen, a wall of tall cabinets with integrated appliances has been kept neutral so that the focus is on the brass-finished natural stone island. The same pattern is repeated in the washbasin where the tadelakt cladding also takes centre stage.

Die Bauherren wollten ein Haus, das als Zufluchtsort vor der Hektik dient, eine wichtige Leitlinie für Menschen, die auf dem Land leben und in die Stadt ziehen. Da sie durch ihr eigenes Möbelgeschäft - Angelique Segaert - mit der Sprache des Designs vertraut waren, nahmen sie Kontakt zu Thaïs Niville auf, und die Affinität war sofort da.

Um den zeitlosen Charakter zu unterstreichen, den die Kunden suchten, wählte die Designerin exklusive Möbelstücke, die die Zeit überdauern, wie die Stühle von Pierre Jeanneret, die Lampe Edifice von Elisa Uberti und den Tisch The line" von Nathalie Deboel. Bei den Oberflächen dominieren natürliche Materialien wie Stein, Eichenholz für den Fußboden und Tadelakt im Bad. Die Textilien in strengem Weiß oder neutralen Farben schaffen einen warmen Kontrast: Wollteppiche und raumhohe Leinenvorhänge filtern das Licht, das durch die großen Fenster im ganzen Haus einfällt. In der Küche wurde eine Wand aus hohen Schränken mit integrierten Geräten neutral gehalten, so dass der Schwerpunkt auf der Insel aus messingfarbenem Naturstein liegt. Das gleiche Muster findet sich im Waschbecken wieder, wo die Tadelaktverkleidung ebenfalls im Mittelpunkt steht.

Les propriétaires souhaitaient une maison où se réfugier à l'abri de l'agitation, une ligne directrice importante pour les personnes ayant vécu à la campagne et déménagé en ville. Familiers avec le langage du design grâce à leur propre magasin de meubles - Angélique Segaert - ils ont contacté Thaïs Niville et l'affinité a été immédiate.

Pour donner l'air intemporel que les clients recherchaient, la designer a choisi des meubles exclusifs qui résistent à l'épreuve du temps, comme les chaises Pierre Jeanneret, la lampe Edifice d'Elisa Uberti et la table « The line » de Nathalie Deboel. Les finitions sont dominées par des matériaux naturels tels que la pierre, le bois de chêne pour le sol et le tadelakt dans la salle de bains. Les textiles d'un blanc strict ou de couleurs neutres créent un contraste de chaleur : les tapis de laine et les rideaux en lin du sol au plafond filtrent la lumière qui entre par les grandes fenêtres de toute la maison. Dans la cuisine, un mur d'armoires hautes avec des appareils électroménagers intégrés est resté neutre afin que l'accent soit mis sur l'îlot en pierre naturelle à finition laiton. Le même motif se retrouve dans le lavabo, où le revêtement en tadelakt occupe également le devant de la scène.

Los propietarios querían una casa para refugiarse del bullicio, una pauta importante tratándose de personas que vivían en el campo y se mudaron a la ciudad. Conocedores del lenguaje del diseño a través de una tienda propia de mobiliario —Angelique Segaert— contactaron con Thaïs Niville y la afinidad fue inmediata.

Para dar el aire atemporal que buscaban los clientes, la diseñadora eligió piezas de mobiliario exclusivas y que resisten al paso del tiempo como las sillas Pierre Jeanneret, la lámpara Edifice de Elisa Uberti o la mesa «The line», de Nathalie Deboel. En los acabados predominan materiales naturales como la piedra, la madera de roble para el suelo y el tadelakt en el baño. Los textiles en estricto color blanco o neutros, generan un contraste de calidez: alfombras de lana, y cortinas de lino que van del techo al suelo filtran la luz que entra por los grandes ventanales en toda la vivienda. En la cocina, una pared de armarios altos con electrodomésticos integrados se ha mantenido neutra para que la atención se centre en la isla de piedra natural con acabados de latón. El mismo patrón se repite en el lavabo donde además cobra protagonismo el revestimiento de *tadelakt*.

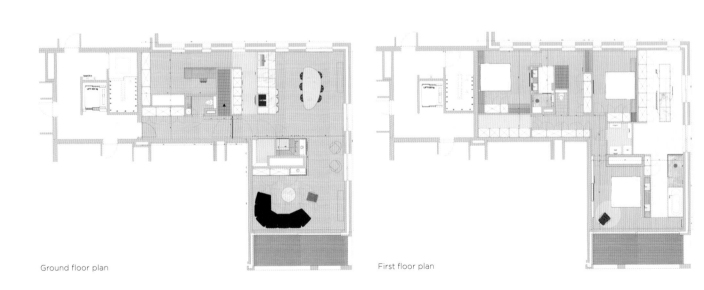

Ground floor plan

First floor plan